men who want to restore their belief that the strength of lifegiver. extends far beyond giving birth and in the extraordinary power of love. The author continually reminds us that the greatest gift that can be gleaned from crimes against humanity, such as the ones committed in Auschwitz, is the courage of witnesses to speak their truth and strengthening our resolve to end bigotry, racism, and hate in order to finally create a world together that is capable of nurturing life."

—Jane Middelton-Moz
author of *Shame and Guilt; Masters of Disguise;*
and *Boiling Point*

Women Surviving Auschwitz

Joy Erlichman Miller, Ph.D.

SiMCHA
P R E S S
An Imprint of Health Communications, Inc.®

Deerfield Beach, Florida
www.simchapress.com

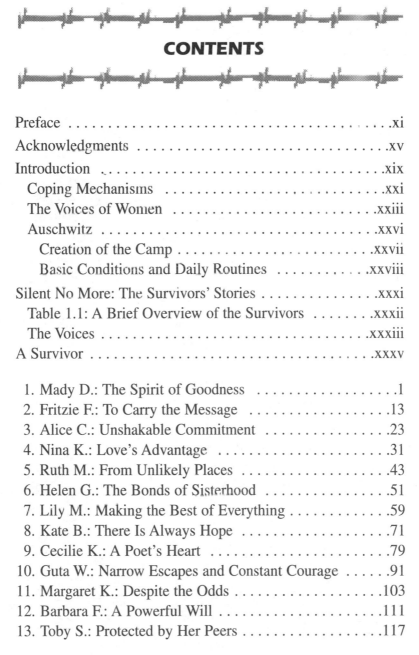

CONTENTS

PREFACE

The purpose of *Love Carried Me Home* is twofold in nature. My first intention is to give "voice" to the female experience, which has been "blended" into the Holocaust literature at large. Secondly, *Love Carried Me Home* focuses on the coping strategies and adaptation mechanisms utilized by women in Auschwitz during the Holocaust.

Within the pages of this book, you will read sixteen women's testimonies and the coping mechanisms they utilized to survive the atrocities and horrors of Auschwitz. The text contains explanations and examples of such emotion-focused coping techniques as affiliation, emotional bonding, distancing, numbing, avoidance and denial, and compares them to such problem-focused strategies as acts of resistance, task-orientated activities, and other forms of manipulating the external environment to minimize the negative consequences of traumatic internment.

Like no other event in history, the Holocaust clearly illustrates the atrocities of genocide: the complete and ultimate annihilation of a particular population. Survival during this horrific time demanded that captives finely hone their skills for coping with the mass traumatization taking place. To mediate their reactions to emotional, physical, economic, cultural and psychological stressors, men and women were forced to use all their defenses and coping strategies to deal with previously unimaginable and devastating horrors.

Although referred to as "gender-neutral," the Holocaust

"voices" used for interpretation, definition and analysis of coping have generally been male. To date, female experiences of the Holocaust have largely been ignored and seen as insignificantly different from those of male counterparts. Male and female voices have been blended together as one, with the assumption that they faced similar, if not identical, circumstances. Yet to gain a meaningful and complete understanding of the Holocaust, it is essential to view the unique coping strategies used by females for survival and adaptation through affiliation and emotional bonding. Women's distinct and poignant voices must be considered in order to fully understand the resiliency of the women who faced the horrors of the Holocaust through their unique strategies and coping mechanisms.

During the twenty-five years I have worked as a psychotherapist, I have witnessed the amazing forces of adaptation utilized by humans to regenerate their own spirits during massive traumatization. My clinical experience often helps me understand the strategies used by survivors to endure the horrors they faced. However, nothing prepared me for the extent of adaptation that was necessary to survive the atrocities of the Holocaust. By gaining an understanding of the strategies utilized, I was able to formulate a broader overview of the tremendous strength we hold in our psychological and spiritual cores. By comprehending the essence of that power, I hoped to gain new clinical resiliency techniques so I could assist others in adapting to massive stressors and trauma in their lives.

In 1994, I pursued my lifelong dream of attaining my doctorate. I always knew my dissertation would include issues related to the Holocaust. My pursuit led me to the United States Holocaust Memorial Museum (USHMM) and to Joan Ringelheim, the director of the museum's oral-history department. After hours of discussion, Dr. Ringelheim helped me formulate a proposal for the investigation of gender-specific research. Dr. Ringelheim shared her own research with me and encouraged me to add to the prevailing literature by utilizing the USHMM's video recordings of female survivors who had been interned in Auschwitz. The research for *Love Carried Me Home* included viewing over seventy-five hours of video testimonies and conducting twenty additional hours of telephone interviews, as well as summarizing the stories of sixteen women from over a thousand pages of transcribed testimonies.

This book begins with a brief overview of the Holocaust and the creation of the Auschwitz Concentration Camp, which includes some exploration of related events that occurred in Eastern Europe in the late 1930s and early 1940s. A brief introduction of the coping strategies used during massive traumatization follows, with references to the prevailing literature related to emotion-focused and problem-focused coping strategies, and emphasis on giving "voice" to the female perspective.

The personal stories of sixteen Auschwitz survivors follow, specifically the first women to give their testimonies to the USHMM at its inception. The survivors' testimonies begin with the youngest to be interred in Auschwitz and concludes with the story of the oldest. The range of experiences will place you right on the path of devastation cut by the Third Reich as it radiated outward from Poland and Germany like a poisonous cancer.

Each of the sixteen testimonies concludes with the survivor's own words as she reflects on the "lessons" she learned during the Holocaust. The women's wisdom, insights and warnings provide an important guide for future generations. After fifty years of reflection, their words, their feelings and their predictions serve to warn future generations. Soon, no witnesses will live to speak of the deliberate, methodical genocide and evil racist philosophies professed during the Third Reich. With no living witnesses to warn us of the destructive potential that arises when prejudice, hatred, greed and evil fuel humanity, the genocidal crimes perpetrated by the Nazis will become mere memories.

Love Carried Me Home is a very powerful chronicle of the lives of these sixteen survivors. With little effort, you will feel transformed and, perhaps, engulfed by the testimonies. The personal narratives will bring you close to each survivor, and you will feel them speaking to you throughout the pages of this book. Please be advised that the material within these pages may create an emotional response. You may find it helpful to read the stories in segments rather than in their entirety. This will make it easier for you to assimilate the information and the emotional impact the stories can prompt.

The stories within these pages are relevant to each of our lives. The survivors teach us that we can endure any trauma if we can touch love: if we go within ourselves and find a reason to continue to live, and to give our lives meaning. The accounts also pay tribute to the powerful psychological technique of "bearing witness" and its importance in the healing process. May the survivors' words throughout these pages serve to ensure that our generation, and our children's children, remember that we must continue to combat hatred, bigotry and racism in our daily lives.

ACKNOWLEDGMENTS

Over forty years ago, I felt traumatized as my Hebrew school teachers spoke of their internment in the Auschwitz Concentration Camp. They made sure we saw the tattoos on their arms, but they never explained how they had gotten them. My teachers made a point of telling us that it was *our* duty to never let "it" happen again, but I still didn't know what "it" was. That was the beginning of years of nightmares and of imaginings of what it was like to be persecuted for being Jewish. It became clear to me, too, that it was *my* personal responsibility to do something to prevent "it" from reoccurring. Eventually, I realized that "it" was the Holocaust. I still wonder if I would have possessed the strength to endure, cope with and survive its atrocities.

The act of writing this book has evolved for me into a transformational healing journey that has led to those who bear witness to the Nazi Holocaust. These survivors have opened their hearts and their souls and shared their deepest guarded thoughts and emotions with me, a woman who needed to know the "truth" of their experiences. Their stories, insights, interpretations and lives will continue to live through those of us who will never forget as we pass the lessons of their lives on to others.

My deepest thanks, respect and love to the brave survivors in my research study—Mady D., Fritzie F., Alice C., Nina K., Ruth M., Helen G., Lily M., Kate B., Cecilie K., Guta W., Margaret K., Barbara F., Toby S., Eva S., Magda B. and Helen W., who have all taught me about the strength of the human spirit and the loving devotion, nurturing and caring of women. You will always hold a special place in my heart and in my soul. You have renewed my spirit and filled it with hope. May God protect you and keep you safe always and forever. Never forget how much I love and respect each of you.

A special thank you to Cecilie, Toby, Magda, Nina, Margaret, Mady, Kate, Guta, Eva, Fritzie and Lily, who have become my distant family. Throughout these past four years you have allowed me into your lives in a special way. You have been my mentors, and I am eternally grateful for all your love and support. Lovingly you have become my special "bubbies" so far away. My deepest appreciation, love and gratitude to Cecilie K., who generously allowed me to use her poems in this work. May her words touch others, as they have touched me!

My gratitude and thanks to Dr. Joan Ringelheim, the Director of Oral History at the United States Holocaust Memorial Museum. My research began with her inspirational work, and my deepest gratitude goes to her for "bailing me out" when I thought the end was in sight. Her assistance and guidance have been invaluable. My thanks also to Travis Roxlau, archivist at the United States Holocaust Memorial Museum, without whom I surely would have gotten lost along the way. And a special thanks to Bonnie Gurewitsch for her expertise and assistance.

Special thanks to my dear friend Marie Stilkind. My editor of over ten years, you once again came to my rescue and gave me the strength to continue my research. As always, your magical editing expertise saved the day. You believed in my passionate journey to share the resilient stories of sixteen women who have changed my life. For that confidence I am forever grateful.

My thanks to Marilee Wilkinson and Sharon Schneider, who so

diligently edited my doctoral dissertation, which was the basis of this work. They were there when I needed them the most. My deepest thanks to my research assistant Marsha Taylor, who has lovingly assisted me in this project.

Miracles do happen! With an artist's touch, Heath Silberfeld's editing transformed this manuscript into a masterpiece. Her dedication, perseverance and friendship were invaluable in the completion of this book. Thank you also to Matthew Diener who diligently assisted in editing this work and bringing it to fruition.

Destiny brought me back to Health Communications and Simcha Press. Your dedicated pursuit of this work has made each moment a miracle in process. Thanks to Kim Weiss and Peter Vegso, who believed in my work. My appreciation to Lisa Drucker and Christine Belleris who assisted through their support and suggestions.

Thanks also to my friends who have stood by me in the last four years while I pursued my dream. Thank you for your encouragement and understanding that friendships endure.

Thanks to my family. First, my parents, Harry and Dee Erlichman, who have always supported me in anything that I dared to achieve. You have always been the wind beneath my wings and the force along my journey. Lovingly, you assured me that I was capable of achieving my wildest dreams and that my only enemy was my fear. Next, thanks to my wonderful husband, John, who always believes in me. With each smile you urge me to continue to follow my path and to believe in my abilities when I am ready to quit. You are my life partner, my best friend and my greatest supporter. And finally, to my remarkable son, Joshua. You are the angel in my life. You fill my life with wonder, laughter, sensitivity and joy, and make me proud of you each moment of the day. Remember to speak of the "truths" to your children so they will never forget what you have witnessed through and learned from these amazing, resilient survivors.

INTRODUCTION

The Holocaust is the name given to the Third Reich's systematic annihilation of approximately 6 million defenseless Jewish men, women and children. The orchestrated genocide that began in Nazi Germany and spread throughout Europe includes all persons murdered in ghettos, concentration camps, extermination death centers and by Einsatzgruppen, or killing squads, of the Nazi reign of terror. The genocide the Nazis waged was relentless toward those people they believed threatened the Third Reich's creation of a superior Aryan nation. The primary population targeted for extermination and annihilation was the Jews. Hitler believed the only means of doing away with the people he referred to as "vermin," the "menacing element" that infected the Reich, was to eliminate every Jew and all things Jewish. One key to this annihilation strategy was the targeting of females, who were the link to future generations of the Jewish population.

The Nazis employed interconnected methods to choke the life from all facets of Jewish existence. This intentional "Final Solution" was fine tuned by targeting Jewish women, for they were the childbearers, the only ones who could ensure the continuity of Jewish life.

Joan Ringelheim, the Director of Oral History at the United States Holocaust Memorial Museum, contends (1993) that there is sound evidence that the survival rate was much lower for Jewish women than for Jewish men. Until 1942 Jewish men may have perished at a quicker rate than females, but statistics illustrate that the overall loss of life during the Shoah was greater for Jewish women. Gender was clearly not a neutral issue for the Nazis. Jewish women were the link to the future of the Jewish nation, and their annihilation was necessary for the completion of Hitler's plan to create a "superior" Aryan nation.

Historically, the voices of the Holocaust—the voices of experience, historical depiction and analysis of the Shoah—have been predominantly those of men. The classic works of our time are the masterpieces of men who have interwoven various disciplines, including writers, psychologists, theologians, philosophers, historians and scholars, as well as those who speak as survivors. These masterpieces are monumental works that have shaped our understanding and influenced our insights, perceptions and interpretations of a systematic genocidal annihilation that is incomprehensible from a "human" perspective. Women's unique voices, however, have rarely been heard, despite the double jeopardy they faced as Jews and as victims of the sexual and maternal violation targeted at them.

One dichotomy that prevailed in Nazi Germany was that European women living outside concentration camps were punished for their infertility while Jewish mothers and female children living within concentration camp walls were murdered for their ability to conceive or were sterilized. Females also faced rape, sexual and physical abuse, forced prostitution, branding, sterilization, mandated abortions and defiling acts of sexual perversion. Women were forced to kill their own babies, as well as other women's children. Some pregnant women were thrown alive into the crematoria. Those with children were generally chosen in death selections. Many were separated from their young, while others were forced to make "choiceless choices" by selecting one child over another in an effort to save at least one child from impending death. Such intricate feminine circumstances demonstrate that women's unique experiences and vulnerabilities merit more attention.

The thoughts, feelings and perspectives of women in Auschwitz reveal distinctions unique to females. By acknowledging these differences, we allow ourselves to benefit from the vital research that has been conducted on gender-related defense mechanisms and survival strategies.

Holocaust researcher Marlene Heinemann (1986) emphasizes gender-specific differences, noting that "to assume that Holocaust literature by men represents the writings of women is to remain blind to the findings of scholarship about the significance of gender in history and literature. Men and women live in different cultural spheres in all societies and have experienced many historical epochs and turning points in quite different ways. Until examination has shown whether men and women experienced and wrote about the Holocaust in the same way, research which implies the 'universality' of men's writing and experiences will be inadequate."

COPING MECHANISMS

Understanding the nature of coping is essential to comprehending people's unique adaptations to the Holocaust. Facing atrocities and horrors beyond comprehension, humans fought to respond, to find meaning, purpose and the will to take another breath to live. To understand human adaptation, one must have a basic overview of coping mechanisms and adaptations employed by survivors who have endured persistent massive trauma.

Noted psychologist Richard S. Lazarus (1991) believes human coping consists of cognitive and behavioral techniques that individuals utilize in their efforts to manage internal and external demands. The two cognitive coping strategies are *problem-focused coping* and *emotion-focused coping*. Simply put, problem-focused coping is action-centered, while emotion-focused coping involves thinking strategies. This premise of Lazarus's work has been utilized as a basis for *Love Carried Me Home* (also see appendix B).

Lazarus's work suggests that problem-focused and emotion-focused coping are utilized at differing degrees of stress. He suggests that at low degrees of stress, the two forms of coping are utilized at identical or similar frequencies. At a moderate degree of perceived stress, problem-focused coping appears to prevail. At high levels of stress, emotion-focused coping appears to be the predominant coping strategy.

Consequently, in some high-stress situations, such as the Holocaust, few opportunities arise to utilize problem-focused coping strategies. Females who were subjected to the massive traumatization of internment in Auschwitz had little opportunity to manipulate their environment, thus they had little opportunity to utilize problem-focused coping.

Emotion-focused coping strategies are by no means passive in nature. It is important to remember that coping strategies are determined by the appraisal one gives to the stress. People typically utilize emotion-focused coping when they conclude that avoidance of reality is more appropriate than direct confrontation. People generally utilize problem-focused coping when an appraisal indicates that something concrete can be accomplished, and use emotion-focused coping when an appraisal implies that nothing can be accomplished.

Some coping strategies are more stable than others. For example, the strategy of numbing is a useful coping tactic, unless it is utilized to an extreme. Many prisoners unconsciously created negative outcomes by overusing numbing, which resulted in disassociation or becoming "the walking dead." Positive outcomes are associated with some coping strategies and negative outcomes with others, based on situational factors. Coping patterns differ with differing stressful encounters and differing individuals.

For example, in chapter 13 you will read the story of Toby S., whose mother took Toby's three-year-old child when they all entered Auschwitz. Upon hearing her child screaming, Toby ran after them, but they had disappeared. Reassured by her cousin that they would be reunited, she believed for nine months that her child and mother were still alive. Even when she witnessed soldiers exterminating the family camp, Toby believed she had to survive for her baby. After nine months of maintaining that her child was alive, Toby learned for certain that her mother and child had been killed the first day they entered Auschwitz. Toby had survived by denying the reality around her. "Don't you see the fire?" she was asked. "Don't you smell the smell? What do you think is there? This is your children. This is your parents." Yet without her emotion-focused coping mechanism, which worked for nine months, would Toby have survived? Many researchers believe such patterns of coping were extremely important for psychological and physical survival during the Shoah.

THE VOICES OF WOMEN

For decades, the unique experiences and coping strategies of female Holocaust survivors were ignored. The voices of survivors were encapsulated into one voice, which was predominantly male. Thus, women's means of coping and adapting in the twentieth century to the genocidal atrocities of the Holocaust were ignored by males who generalized the experiences of all who bore witness. However, survivors, researchers and historians such as Charlotte Delbo (1992, 1993), Marlene Heinemann (1986), Isabella Leitner (1985, 1994), Joan Ringelheim (1984, 1985, 1993), Carol Rittner (1993), Nechama Tec (1986) and Bonnie Gurewitsch (1998) have discussed the Shoah from a different perspective, which focuses on the feelings, coping strategies and traumas that express the "invisible female voice."

Sadly, many female Holocaust researchers and survivors have been severely criticized for their gender-related conclusions. Many female survivors and scholars have suggested the importance of relational bonding as an essential coping strategy for female Holocaust survivors. The opposition has argued that gender-specific focusing has the potential to denigrate the Holocaust, reducing it to sexism and detracting from the experiences of the survivors. Opponents believe that those perpetrating the genocide and atrocities of the Third Reich counted Jews as Jews, not as men, women or children.

Viktor Frankl, one of the most noted Holocaust survivors, states (1984, 1988) that survivors of the Holocaust identified with a "meaning or will to survive" as a means of coping. Gender-based researcher Sondra Rappaport's (1991) work on the coping strategies and methods of adaptation used by Holocaust survivors suggests that women used different forms of coping techniques to develop "meaning" needed for survival. Her work reveals that women tended to cope by bonding emotionally to others, while men coped by focusing on tasks. Deborah Belle (cited in Alan Monat and Richard S. Lazarus 1991) agrees that women value relationships and define themselves in terms of their relationships, and that involvement in supportive human relationships protects stressed individuals from physical and mental-health concerns.

Generally, women seek support more readily than males during times of stress. For instance, in chapter 10 you will read about Guta W., who beseeched not only a German woman guard for help to save her mother, but Eichmann himself. Guta knew no fear in her attempts to save her mother. Women also have shown a propensity to seek out more formal and informal sources of support and affiliation than males during stress.

Another gender-specific difference relates to the loss of loved ones. At such times, women Holocaust survivors appear to have been less vulnerable than male counterparts due to the support and encouragement they received from fellow prisoners. The assistance of other women helped maintain women's emotional strength and resiliency. The bonds created with others helped women cope with the dehumanizing acts of the Nazi regime.

Female survivors' narratives bear witness to their own personal interpretations of "meaning" and moral choices, but women's decisions are clearly based on meaning, which includes a dimension of concern and caring for others whom they value. The personal stories within this book make it clear that establishing and creating binding relationships was a critical factor for many survivors. Reestablishing a new community or family by bonding with other women assisted the surviving prisoners in creating a reason to live (see appendix A, "The Findings").

It is important to note, however, that nearly all Auschwitz victims knew that their survival had something to do with an element of luck or chance. Many believe that luck had more to do with their survival than anything within their own control.

Despite the massive numbers of females murdered, surviving Jewish women continue to bear witness and celebrate their ability to survive. Through oral histories, narratives and autobiographies, their personal stories celebrate the "meaning" that kept them ever striving to survive despite insurmountable odds.

Following a brief description of Auschwitz on the following pages, the stories in this book bear witness to the resiliency of sixteen female survivors. Whether due to luck, technical skills, non-Jewish appearance, a hope of reunion, faith, humor, personal resistance, or the assistance of or through a relationship with another, these women survived, holding on valiantly to the will to live!

AUSCHWITZ

Auschwitz has become synonymous with Nazi tyranny, systematic dehumanization and annihilation, torturous daily labor, and, ultimately, the genocide of over six million Jews during the Holocaust. No other event in modern history has been marked with such a systematic approach to obliterating a targeted population. The Auschwitz Concentration Camp has become an accepted metaphor for the demonic human dark side that perpetrated a degree of genocide beyond human comprehension. In Auschwitz, the Nazis implemented unique methods of physical and psychological torture and dehumanization and destruction of the human spirit.

The Auschwitz-Birkenau complex served as a forced labor camp, as well as an extermination center, from May 1940 through January 27, 1945. Auschwitz was not the first Nazi concentration camp to also serve as a death camp, but it remains the most infamous. Built in Oswiecim, Poland, fifty kilometers southwest of Krakow, it was the largest concentration-camp complex, with over forty subcamps, or satellite camps, under its auspices. Over 450,000 men and women were incarcerated, registered and numbered within the camp complex, and records indicate that over 200,000 registered prisoners perished there as part of Hitler's "Final Solution." According to the most reliable estimates, more than one million more Jews were murdered in the gas chambers upon arrival at Auschwitz before being processed and registered (Gutman and Berenbaum 1994).

Creation of the Camp

On April 18, 1940, SS Hauptsturmführcr Rudolf Höss visited Oswiecim and reported to SS Reichsführer Heinrich Himmler concerning the advantages of this site as a concentration-camp and extermination-camp complex. On April 27, 1940, Himmler ordered the establishment of the camp and named Höss the commandant of the complex. Originally, they intended Auschwitz to serve as a concentration camp for political prisoners, mainly Polish dissidents, but with the additional conquests of the Third Reich, as well as the determination of Hitler's policy of deportation and annihilation of "undesirables," the camp's prisoner population grew quickly, exceeding by far the original plan for the camp.

The first prisoners to be sent to Auschwitz were a group of 728 political prisoners, including five Jews. They arrived from Tarnow, Poland, on June 14, 1940, and Czech, Soviet and Yugoslavian prisoners soon joined them. Himmler had originally classified the camp in the same category as Dachau and Sachsenhausen, which together were considered a complex for those whose offenses were light and correctable. With the ever-increasing transport of prisoners, construction of Birkenau, which later became Auschwitz II, started in October 1941. With the proclamation of Hitler's "Final Solution of the Jewish question" at the Wannsee Conference in 1942, Auschwitz was designated as the primary location for the extermination of Jews.

In February 1942, the first transport composed entirely of Jews arrived at the gates of Auschwitz. Jews were brought from almost every part of Europe. Crammed inhumanely into cattle cars, they traveled for days without sanitary facilities and without food or water. They were met at Auschwitz by Selektion (selection) doctors, headed by Josef Mengele, who decided, based on appearance and age, who was fit for work and who would be sent to the awaiting gas chambers. Those not murdered immediately were used as slave labor within the camp complex. Those deemed "unfit" (children, pregnant women and the elderly) were sent to their deaths amid intense screaming upon separation from family, friends and loved ones. "Few (of the survivors) lived longer than six months; they died from starvation, disease, the rigors of hard labor, beatings, torture and summary execution—by shooting, hanging or gassing" (Swiebocka 1993).

Basic Conditions and Daily Routines

In a dehumanizing and degrading process, the prisoners placed in the line chosen for "life" were forced to remove all clothing and were shaved of all hair. They were then registered and tattooed on a forearm, suggesting their entrance date to the camp. Prisoners "selected" to live were crammed into "blocks," barracks with wooden bunks infested with lice. Sanitary facilities were primitive, and prisoners were not allowed to care for daily elimination needs. Soiled clothes filled with lice were distributed and purposely given in the wrong size. Many times prisoners were forced to run naked from barracks to delousing showers and then to parade in front of prison doctors and guards for Selektion (selection).

Each day faded into another. The roll call at 4:30 each morning was not completed until every single prisoner was accounted for by the Kapos (prisoners acting as police). The punishment for a missing person or an escapee might be multiple killings of other prisoners, inhumane beatings or hangings performed in front of the remaining traumatized prisoners. Even dead bodies had to be presented for accounting before completion of the roll call. As a means of additional torture for prisoners, the Appells (roll calls) sometimes took up to nineteen hours in subzero temperatures. Upon completion of roll call, the masses received a 300-gram piece of bread, a pat of lard and watery coffee. The morning food allotment was followed by the prisoners being marched, many times to German music, to strenuous slave labor at factories, mines and road-construction sites. No rest was allowed, and those who did not comply were beaten, shot or left to die from exhaustion. "Night brought little rest from the tortures of the day. The bunks were so overcrowded that prisoners were unable to move, and fleas and lice made rest impossible" (Swiebocka 1993).

Of the 1.5 million people taken to Auschwitz, many were not registered and were killed immediately. Of the approximately 405,000 prisoners registered and assigned numbers upon arrival, estimates assert that 200,000 perished prior to liberation. On January 18, 1945, the final roll call in Auschwitz and auxiliary camps accounted for 64,000 prisoners, including just over 16,000 women. Approximately 6,000 prisoners remained in Auschwitz during the winter and spring of 1945, while 58,000 made a "forced death march" through Austria and Germany.

On January 27, 1945, at 9:00 A.M., a Russian soldier appeared in Monowitz, one of the Auschwitz auxiliary camps. That afternoon the Red Army entered Birkenau and Auschwitz's main camp and liberation, at long last, began.

SILENT NO MORE:
THE SURVIVORS' STORIES

In the following chapters, you will read the miraculous stories of sixteen women who survived the Auschwitz Concentration Camp. You will learn about each survivor's interpretation of the rise of anti-Semitism, the effects of the rise of Hitler, ghettoization, the effects upon family and community, internment, liberation, and life after the war. In addition, you will learn the unique coping strategies utilized by each survivor to remain resilient during her struggle for survival. For ten of our survivors, you will also find a condensation of a telephone interview in which the survivor summarized her personal insights about internment and her coping strategies for survival in Auschwitz.

The survivors' testimonies are part of a collection produced for use in the permanent exhibits at the United States Holocaust Memorial Museum in Washington, D.C. These women represent the geographic areas of Europe that were heavily impacted in the early years of Nazi occupation, racial legislation, immigration, and deportation of Jews and "undesirables" to ghettos and concentration camps. The survivors cited have varying dates of birth that are concurrent with rising European anti-Semitism, the increasing popularity of racist ideologies, and the rise of Hitler's influence and power during the Third Reich. The years of internment for women are limited because women were not sent in large numbers to Auschwitz. When sent, women were generally "liquidated" immediately.

TABLE 1.1: A BRIEF OVERVIEW OF THE SURVIVORS

Name	Year of Birth	Country of Origin	Year of Arrival in Auschwitz	Age Upon Arrival
Madeline (Mady) D.	1930	Czechoslovakia	1944	14
Fritzie F.	1929	Czechoslovakia	1944	15
Alice C.	1929	Hungary	1944	15
Nina K.	1929	Poland	1943 (January)	13
Ruth M.	1929	Germany	1943 (April)	13
Helen G.	1928	Czechoslovakia	1944	16
Lily M.	1928	Belgium	1944 (Spring)	15 (almost 16)
Kate B.	1927	Hungary	1944 (May)	17
Cecilie K.	1925	Czechoslovakia	1944 (May)	19
Guta W.	1924	Poland	1944	20
Margaret K.	1923	Germany	1942	19
Barbara F.	1920	Romania	1944	24
Toby S.	1920	Romania	1944 (Spring)	24
Eva S.	1919	Poland	1943	24
Magda B.	1916	Slovakia	1942 (June)	26
Helen W.	1909	Germany	1944	35

The Voices

The young children and the babies that were taken out of mothers' arms and put onto these trucks; and the mothers running after them. And the crying and the screaming, "My baby!" And they were told they would see them later. . . . The old people, the cripples—whoever couldn't walk, these were put on trucks. The young people needed to line up. Women and men were separated, as were children. My mother and I stood on the same line when they told us to line up, and then they started to call age. Mother was a young woman. They called, "Age!" And I told my mother she stood in the wrong line.

My mother went into another line. I found out several hours later that the line she went in went directly to the gas chambers. (Crying) I'm sorry.

How does one describe the walking into Auschwitz, the . . . the smell? And someone pointing out to you that those are gas chambers, that your parents went up in smoke? When I asked, "When will I see my mother?" I was shown the smoke. How do I describe fear? How do I describe hunger to someone that has probably had breakfast and lunch today? Or even if you're dieting, or even if you're fasting for a day. I think hunger is when the pit of your stomach hurts. When you would sell your soul for a potato or a slice of bread. How do I describe living with the lice in your clothes, on your body? The stink. The fear. The selections. The Appells. The being told when to go to the toilet, not when you needed to use it. The using of the morning coffee to wash your face with. Mengele. And mostly, mostly death and the gas chambers.

Archival oral testimony of Fritzie F.
United States Holocaust Memorial Museum

A Survivor

A survivor wears nice clothes with a matching smile, trying to recapture the forgotten pleasures of life, but is unable fully to enjoy anything.

A survivor will go on vacation and, while watching a show, will picture her mother, holding her grandson in her arms, gasping for breath.

A survivor will read about a fire and desperately hope that her brother had died from the fumes before the flames reached him.

A survivor will think of her sister with her three dead children and inhale the gas to feel the gasping agony of their deaths.

A survivor will go to a party and feel alone.

A survivor appears quiet but is screaming within.

A survivor will make large weddings, with many guests, but the ones she wants most will never arrive.

A survivor will go to a funeral and cry, not for the deceased but for the ones that were never buried.

A survivor will reach out to you but not let you get close, for you remind her of what she could have been, but will never be.

A survivor is at ease only with other survivors.

A survivor is broken in spirit, but pretends to be like you.

A survivor is a wife, mother, friend, neighbor, yet nobody really knows her.

A survivor is a restless tortured person; she can only enjoy her children. Yet it is not easy to be the children of a survivor, for she expects the impossible of them—to be constantly happy, to do and learn all the things denied to her.

A survivor will awaken in a sweat from her nightmares, unable to sleep again. In vain does she chase the ghosts from her bedside, but they remain her guests for the remainder of the night.

A survivor has no fear of death, for peace is its reward.

Cecilie Klein, *Sentenced to Live*

1

Mady D.
The Spirit of Goodness

adeline (Mady) D. was born on April 29, 1930, in Berehovo, Czechoslovakia. Within this small city, she and her older brother were raised in a tight-knit, middle-income family. Mady's father was a businessman who worked out of his home.

Brought up in a family that valued education, Mady received both formal schooling during the day and religious education in the late afternoon. In 1938 anti-Semitic sentiment was increasing in her world. Her father was an avid reader of the newspaper and listened to news of world events on the radio. The family heard about what was happening in Poland but for the most part believed that the reports were nothing more than tales of horror that had been exaggerated to scare the Jews. For the most part, the Jewish community disregarded the stories.

In November 1938, Germany rewarded Hungary by annexing territory to Hungary. Mady's hometown of Berehovo was part of this annexation. Educational opportunities began to dwindle as teachers became increasingly anti-Semitic. Jewish doctors and lawyers were not allowed to practice their professions, and Jewish doctors were limited to treating Jewish patients. Businesses were slowly taken over by the Hungarian government and Aryan businessmen.

In March 1944, Hitler invaded Hungary. Mady was thirteen years old. All Jews were ordered to wear a yellow, six-pointed Star of David on the fronts and backs of their garments, a symbol that designated them as second-class citizens. In April of that year, Jews, including Mady and her family, were rounded up and told to leave their homes with only a small satchel of belongings. While forced to live in a small ghetto with no beds or cots, the families lived in covered areas similar to market stalls or carports.

After being coerced into giving all valuables and money to the

German authorities, Mady's father narrowly escaped being shot when some forgotten money was discovered in one of his vest pockets. This occurred on Mady's fourteenth birthday, and she recalled that it was one of the happiest moments of her life when her father was released and not shot, as threatened, by the Germans.

Mady observed that the Hungarian police were much more brutal than the Germans and that they were rewarded for beatings and cruelty to Jewish prisoners. "We didn't have any guns. We had nothing to protect ourselves with. So when we were herded out of our homes and into this ghetto, all we had with us (was) that little change of clothing and nothing else. So we had no way of protecting (ourselves) and we had no way . . . it just made no . . . no sense to really protect (ourselves) although we tried, and those that did were beaten up something terrible. But we had no way of protecting against all these guns and against these SS and against these soldiers . . . you know, the police."

About two weeks later the Nazis liquidated the ghetto and moved Mady and her family in cattle cars to an unknown destination. Countless people died in the cattle cars while packed into cramped quarters with no food or sanitation. After three days and three nights, the train stopped at the gates of Auschwitz. Mady vividly remembered entering the camp in the dark, smelling the odor that filled the air and seeing the flames in the distance. "The odor that was coming in through those little windows into those cattle cars was horrible. We didn't know what that was. It was burning, like burning flesh, but who would . . . whose mind would enter something like this?"

The group heard howling dogs and German voices as they waited in the train until daybreak. When the cattle-car doors opened, they saw electrified barbed-wire fences. People in German uniforms and people in striped uniforms began pulling them off the trains. "We just saw them take off these dead people, and we were still to stand in line there because the police—I mean the SS—at this point already were there with their police dogs and we were standing there because nobody dared to move. They (would) just release the dogs, who tore people apart."

Men and women were separated while people in striped uniforms whispered to the group that they were in Auschwitz where "all your parents and your grandparents and your babies were killed and will be killed." The prisoners were falsely reassured by the SS—told to stay calm and that they would be cared for—while the striped-uniform inmates warned them that they would never make it out of Auschwitz alive.

Mady's father and brother were taken to one side and Mady and her mother to another line, where guards directed them along a ramp. The healthier people were separated from the older people and little children.

"But my mother was a very, very intelligent woman. . . . And when she saw this well-dressed officer who had a couple of . . . assistants near him . . . and when she saw that this officer was directing the older people to go in one direction and the younger people in the other direction, she must have had some kind of intuition." She pinched Mady's cheeks and instructed her to stand tall so she would look healthy. In perfect German, Mady's mother informed the officer, who happened to be Dr. Josef Mengele, that she was forty-three and that Mady was fourteen. Mady and her mother were then directed to the line of those who would live and were sent to the showers.

Mady, along with the rest of the group, was told to enter the showers for washing and disinfection. Unknown to the survivors, the other group was being exterminated in the gas chambers nearby. All head and body hair was shaven after the women exited the showers. Mady remembered the women's humiliation as they stood naked, trying to cover their bodies, while men shaved them. Completely shaven, each woman was given a large gray shirtdress and exited the showers. People were unable to recognize their now-bald family members and had to call out names to find their missing relatives. Women were moved to a crowded barracks with wooden sleeping bunks and packed into the space so tightly that it was impossible for anyone to turn over.

To counter their dehydration the next day, many people grabbed desperately for a little water from puddles or a fountain, not knowing that the water supply was contaminated from the fluids of the dead seeping underground into the water system. The water poisoned some and others became very sick and unable to stand, and the women in the roll-call lines assisted each other to create the illusion that they were strong enough to continue through the day.

Mady and her mother, having been selected by Mengele, were transferred one week later to a work-camp ammunition factory in Breslau (Mady has always believed this was because her mother was a blue-eyed blonde who spoke fluent German). The work camp utilized approximately five hundred to six hundred women, most from Poland, who survived longer than average because they were particularly strong and previously hardened by harsh conditions. The majority of these Polish women had been ghettoized or imprisoned in other concentration camp settings for many years. All were awakened each day at 5:00 in the morning, counted, and given a small piece of moldy, dark bread and some lukewarm brown water. Her mother was fearful for Mady's health and rationed the bread during the day. Mady discovered later that her mother had been giving Mady a portion of her own bread to increase the chances of her daughter's survival. Mady said her mother would do anything possible to protect her daughter from harm and suffering. On many occasions Mady's mother encouraged her to try harder to continue working: "Try. Make believe you are doing it even if you . . . you're unable to. . . . Try a little harder. . . . Maybe we'll get out of here soon. Maybe we're gonna see your father and brother. . . . Maybe we'll see your grandparents and aunts and uncles when we come back. . . . Just hold on a little bit longer."

Mady knew they were making parts used in bomb settings for airplanes and other pieces of ammunition but that they had no choice except to do as they were told. "And we were working in this factory and you have to understand what we were . . . what we had to do in order to survive because whoever resisted was killed on the spot so there was no if . . . it was a choice. Either to live or to die. If you did what you were told, then temporarily you know that you are alive. . . . We had to make . . . help manufacture that if we wanted to survive. And human nature is very funny. We all want to live. The oldest and the sickest person in this world wants to go on living. That is human nature."

Mady and her mother remained in a women's camp called Peterswaldau (part of Gross-Rosen) for almost one year while working in the ammunition factory. Near the end of the war, no supplies were available to manufacture ammunition, so the workers were forced to dig foxholes. "I must have weighed maybe fifty or sixty pounds. I was like a skeleton . . . and whoever couldn't perform, they just killed."

One morning, the small camp was especially quiet, and the prisoners soon learned that the SS had fled during the night (May 8, 1945). Russian solders liberated the group and cared for the prisoners for two or three weeks.

Mady and her mother attempted to regain their strength so

they could return to their family. Hoping that father and husband, brother and son, would still be alive, mother and daughter traveled home to discover that their neighbors had taken their home, their business and all their valuables. While waiting in their hometown, hoping to reunite with their family, Mady and her mother were told that both the men had perished in a labor camp and that Mady's father had witnessed the death of his son and given up all hope when he was told that the Germans had killed all the women. Mady later discovered that only three of her mother's eight siblings had survived, along with four of her cousins.

Mady and her mother stayed in a displaced persons' camp for four years and then emigrated to the United States on March 9, 1949, where they lived with Mady's aunt and uncle in Pittsburgh, Pennsylvania. A year later Mady and her mother moved to New York City to be in a larger Jewish community. Mady suffered from post-traumatic stress disorder (fear, nightmares, vomiting) for a number of years. "I was afraid that the Nazis were still out there. I was having nightmares . . . for many years. I was still reliving everything. The trip to Auschwitz, the beatings, the killings, the dead people taken off the train . . . the dogs that were released and jumped on people . . . and tore them apart."

At age nineteen, Mady met a young man who encouraged her to return to school and accompanied her to the first classes at Theodore Roosevelt High School. She met another Holocaust survivor at night school and married him six months later in 1956, and their family grew to include two sons and two grandchildren.

Mady continued her education and later became an interior decorator. Her mother remarried, then died of cancer in 1978. Mady has been very active in the activities of the Holocaust

Memorial Museum Houston and is one of four survivors who created a permanent exhibit there. She also has been part of the museum's speaker's bureau since 1980.

In 2000, Mady attended "The Gathering of Survivors" in Washington, D.C. She is dedicated to teaching the lessons of the Shoah and often quotes George Santayana, an American philosopher: "Those who cannot remember the past are condemned to repeat it."

HOW MADY D. COPED

Affiliation with her mother and believing that she would be reunited with her family played a large part in Mady's ability to cope emotionally with her early Holocaust experiences. Mady's mother, always protective of her daughter and extremely intuitive, was very supportive of and caring toward her daughter. Mady's mother was a driving force in Mady's coping and adaptation, constantly pushing her to try harder, to think of the eventual reunion with loved ones, to stay healthy and emotionally strong. Mother also sustained daughter by cautiously rationing her food supply, as well as adding to the quantity by giving portions of her own food to her young daughter without Mady knowing about it.

Mady put her emotion-focused coping skills to good use in counseling her mother after they learned of the death of their father/husband and brother/son. Mady remembered when her mother wanted to commit suicide because she felt she had no reason to live: "I had just turned fifteen. I was so young. I wanted to go on and see if there is something beautiful in this world . . . if there are some good things in people . . . if there are some good things in this world where people lived . . . not just suffering and ugliness that we have seen. I just wanted to go on and see some goodness and beauty. And she told me that if I wanted to go on living, her duty as a mother was to go on to help me survive and go on."

The hope and belief that one day they would be reunited with their family in Czechoslovakia gave Mady and her mother a purpose and a will to survive despite the atrocities of Auschwitz and the work camp. Mady remarked, "What kept us alive all this time was thinking about and dreaming about them and hoping that we will meet again, that they'll survive as well. And then we'll be one happy family again. And this is what my mother kept me alive with."

Mady mentioned no problem-focused coping strategies. It was obvious in her testimony that the ability to manipulate the environment was restricted and that the methodology to live from one day to another focused on helping each other and believing that tomorrow would bring an end to their trauma.

PHONE INTERVIEW WITH MADY D.

Mady was very insistent that she had no technique for coping or surviving, that there was no technique or active strategy that anyone could use to enhance their chances of survival. Much of what occurred was due basically to luck. The human drive to live was the determining force in her survival, and Mady stated that it was her mother and others who protected her during times of adversity: "We were still human beings . . . we still tried to help each other . . . survive the atrocities of the concentration camp and working labor camps. We just tried to hold on to each other as much as we could." At any time, Mady stated, she could choose suicide and throw herself against electrified wire fencing, but she maintained her hope. Her mother's will and her constant encouragement drove Mady each day to continue to live with the hope of being reunited with her family.

Despite the humiliation, the atrocities and the horrors, Mady very badly wanted to live. She believed she used fantasy as a powerful tool to escape from the reality of the atrocities. In her fantasies and dreams, she imagined she would return to her homeland and to a normal life with her family after the war.

Through the Eyes of Mady D.

I go from school to school and from organization to organization and from church to church and talk to all the groups. When someone is being persecuted for whatever reason (I tell them) to help and to speak up . . . to remember the past and hope to make a better life for the future. Mankind must learn to live together in peace, and harmony and respect each other. . . . It is important that we as survivors "tell them about the Holocaust, our experiences, and tell them (schoolchildren) to read about the past and learn about it, and try in their lifetimes (to) stop things like this from happening. And it is up to the young people . . . today's generation can prevent something like this from happening again . . . (they must) be aware and watchful and care about people. And when somebody is being persecuted for whatever reason to help, and speak up, and remember the past and make a better life for the future.

2

Fritzie F.
To Carry the Message

ritzie F. was born in 1929 in Klucarky, Czechoslovakia, which was near the town of Munkacs. Her home was in a very small village with a few Jewish families who were very close to one another. A comfortable mixing of Jews and non-Jews populated her community. "We lived in peace with our neighbors . . . my very best friends were non-Jewish as well as Jewish."

Fritzie's father emigrated to the United States after the Great Depression of 1929 and did not have time to arrange for his family's emigration before the outbreak of war and the Nazi occupation. U.S. immigration policy was extremely strict at that time, and immigration of a family was permitted only when an "alien resident" could illustrate financial stability for the family in America. Fritzie had few memories of her father and remembered that her mother was afraid, ironically, to take her remaining family to the United States during the early 1940s because of the dangers related to crossing the Atlantic in wartime.

Fritzie heard horror stories about Jews being persecuted in Poland and Germany in 1939 and knew that her family had hidden many young Jews and assisted in their escape into parts of Czechoslovakia. She remembered helping her grandfather with underground activities in an effort to assist escaping Jews who soon would be persecuted under the occupation of the Third Reich. "I recall hiding many of these young Jewish people who would come and putting them into wagons and covering them with straw and whatever and taking them to parts of Czechoslovakia, to different towns."

Fritzie's first recollection of the effects of occupation was of her schoolteacher denying her access to her continued education. The teacher told Fritzie that she was no longer allowed to attend the school because she was Jewish.

"A teacher—who was my teacher—who took out a white handkerchief from his pocket the week before to wipe a smudge off my face, turned to me one day and told me I must not come to school anymore." Within a day's time, Jews were labeled as different, inferior, and in need of segregation and regulation. The government established rules for access to educational institutions, time limits for shopping or walking on public streets or working, bans for sitting on public benches, and mandates for wearing a yellow star to indicate that one was Jewish. Each day brought about another legislated rule, another edict, or a new law to restrict freedom and dignity.

"If someone came toward someone who was not a Jew, the Jew needed to step off the sidewalk to allow the next person—who of course was not Jewish—to walk by. I recall our neighbors turning their backs on us. Spitting on us. Neighbors who lived in peace with us, who were our friends the week before."

In March 1944 the Jews were told to gather their belongings for relocation in a ghetto in their own town. They quickly realized they had mistakenly believed the lies of those they had trusted. Though hopeful they would be relocated in a "safe place," they soon realized that their fate led to imprisonment. "I will never understand how one human—a neighbor, a friend—can turn against you . . . a person who has lived with you in peace, who watched you being born, who has gone to school with you, who knows your family and knows your life history . . . But, nevertheless, that's what they did."

The SS had converted the town grammar school into the ghetto lodging and brought guards and dogs to herd the

Jews into this building and force them to live in crowded conditions. The Germans came each day and ordered the young Jews to perform forced labor. Most were returned each night until they were all cleared from the ghetto in 1944 and placed on a cattle car heading to Auschwitz.

No room was available for sitting down for three days in the overcrowded cattle car heading to an unknown destination. Each day guards pushed a bucket of water into the car for the prisoners to divide for drinking. Another bucket was used as a public toilet. Fritzie reflected upon the impossibility of explaining the "dignity that is taken away from you when you need to use a bucket as a toilet in the middle of a compartment on a train, in front of everyone. About sharing water with every single person . . . about the mothers holding on to hungry children who cried. The stink. The fear. It's strange, fear gives out a certain smell. And that mixed with the open bucket—it's a smell I don't believe one can ever forget."

Fritzie's first sights when she entered Auschwitz were barking dogs, guards with whips and multitudes of humans screaming in despair. People were beaten and forced into separate lines. Babies were ripped from their mothers' arms. Children were separated from parents, husbands from wives and family from family.

Just after being advised by another prisoner to say that she was older than her age, Fritzie was told to stand in a line next to others. "They walked among us, and in Yiddish they would whisper, 'You're fifteen. Remember you're fifteen.'" Fritzie told her mother to move to a different line during the chaos. Thus she went into the line of "life" and, tragically, her mother went into the line of "death." Later Fritzie discovered that her two brothers had gone directly to the gas chambers.

Upon asking when she would see her mother, she was shown the smoke coming from the chimney and told it was her mother.

Fritzie's aunt was a source of great emotional support throughout their internment, and she survived the months at Auschwitz only with her aunt's assistance. Stories of Mengele, selections, daily uncertainty, torture and endless roll calls were prominent in her testimony. She accomplished her survival with emotion-focused coping and adaptation, which centered on hope and affiliation.

"You never knew when your turn was going to come. But I think the struggle to survive is in all of us. And . . . none of us really know the kind of energy we put in every day to survive, unless we're forced with this. My thought was always of tomorrow. And I believe that's what . . . maybe youth . . . but my hope was always of tomorrow."

After nearly nine months of internment, Fritzie's barrack was emptied and she was marched toward the gas chambers. Her aunt was put on a truck to be sent away. Her aunt pleaded with an SS guard to have Fritzie join her on the truck. "I was literally in the door of the gas chamber. Six of us were pulled out of line. I will never know the reason why. Our small group was pulled out and put onto another truck, with several other women, to go to work in a factory. . . . I was the youngest of six hundred women . . . I was their hope . . . I was their hope to carry the message to the world."

Because of the Allies' approach, prisoners were forced to move eastward on a death march. They marched through streets covered, literally, with bodies. People were dropping dead from hunger, from disease, from exhaustion or because they had given up hope. During that forced march in 1945,

Fritzie and a friend ran into the forest and escaped until the Russians liberated them. Upon returning to her old home, Fritzie contacted her father in the United States, and she joined him in 1947.

Even as a teenager, Fritzie had difficulty facing her memories of the Holocaust. "So I had taken all of my memories and put them in a little box, and put them on the very bottom of my brain. Closed the box never to be taken out, never to be examined. This is how I lived for many years. This is how I handled my past."

Fritzie suffered from post-traumatic stress disorder and never discussed the Holocaust with anyone: "It was taboo." She would not associate with survivors, and in 1949 she married an American marine who knew only that she was a survivor. Interestingly, Fritzie's husband was also a prisoner of war during the Holocaust, held captive by Japan on Wake Island.

Fritzie and her husband have had one son and two grandchildren. In the mid-1980s, Fritzie's son asked her to read a newspaper article that had been submitted by the Holocaust Foundation of Illinois. The article asked for survivors to come forward to record their stories. Fritzie's son pleaded with her to share her story for preservation by her family and future generations. Knowing her son would not take "no" for an answer, Fritzie gave her testimony to various survivor groups, including the United States Holocaust Memorial Museum.

After she recorded her testimony, Fritzie became very active as a volunteer, speaker and fundraiser for the United States Holocaust Memorial Museum in Washington, D.C. She has also been active with the Midwest Region Holocaust Memorial Foundation in Illinois and has served on its board of directors. She speaks on behalf of the Skokie Holocaust Memorial Foundation of Illinois and to many schoolchildren about the lessons of the Holocaust. She is always the host and speaker at a Yom Hashoah/Day of Remembrance breakfast initiated by Mayor Richard Daley Jr. and attended by thousands of Chicago-area public-school students.

Fritzie has also been very influential in bringing educational exhibits from the United States Holocaust Memorial Museum to the Chicago area and continues her dedicated goal of ensuring the Midwest chapter leads the fund-raising campaign in the country.

Fritzie's story has also been quoted in Michael Berenbaum's *The World Must Know: The History of the Holocaust as Told in the U.S. Holocaust Memorial Museum,* and currently numerous authors are soliciting the rights to tell the story of her life and that of her husband. Recently, Fritzie helped host a tour to Auschwitz and Eastern Europe with the United States Holocaust Memorial Museum.

HOW FRITZIE F. COPED

Fritzie F.'s emotion-focused coping included maintaining hope and affiliation with others. "None of us really know the kind of energy we put in every day to survive, unless we're faced with this. . . . My thoughts were always of tomorrow." Fritzie's comments within her testimony suggest that she believed the future would be better and that her affiliations with others (her aunt and the six hundred women in the working camp) and her caring and nurturing of others provided the basis for her emotion-focused coping. Her testimony mentioned no problem-focused coping strategies. This may be due to Fritzie's youth and the fact that others cared for and protected her.

However, Fritzie's comments concerning her postwar years suggested that she was affected with post-traumatic stress disorder. She stated that she used problem-focused and emotion-focused coping to deal with her life after immigration to the United States. "I could not live with my memories of what had happened. I couldn't handle them." Her statements illustrated repression, denial and avoidance, which are techniques of emotion-focused coping. Her isolation from other survivors, her abstinence from Jewish organizations, her refusal to discuss anything related to her experiences in the Holocaust, and her avoidance of any questions asked by others concerning her experiences illustrate problem-focused coping strategies.

"These things we don't talk about," she recollected in her testimony. "This is how I lived for many years. This was my way." Researchers call this the "conspiracy of silence."

Through the Eyes of Fritzie F.

They tell us Hitler did this. Did Hitler really do this by himself? Are we forgetting the soldiers that gathered us? The people that took care of the ghettos? The people that drove the trains to Treblinka and other places? The men and women who were the guards in Auschwitz Concentration Camp? Our neighbors that turned us in? Are we forgetting all of that? Hitler didn't do it himself. Hitler had lots of help. What about these men that were the guards in the camps, that would go home at night to play with their children and listen to their music and hug their wives while they were killing our parents and our sisters and brothers? Did they keep a secret? Can they keep a secret? How many people can keep a secret? We were told that they didn't know. What about all the people who lived in the towns around Auschwitz and other concentration camps, who saw the flames day in and day out? Who smelled the stink of the bodies burn-ing, day in and day out? What about all the people who saw the trains passing by, and the people begging for water, for food to give to their babies?

3

Alice C.
Unshakable Commitment

lice C. was born in 1929 in Budapest, Hungary. Her childhood and community were very family-oriented. Her grandfather was a self-made industrialist, a leader within the Jewish community. Her sister, Edith, was two and a half years older and her two brothers were younger. Alice "mothered" and cared for her youngest brother.

Jewish visitors came to Budapest and related what was happening with the German occupation, but Alice's family did not believe that such atrocities could occur in their country. "We always felt so very protected . . . maybe that happens in Poland, in Czechoslovakia. But Hungary is civilized. We are very good taxpayers. They need us here. It will not happen. And then one day, they (Germans) say that you pack up twenty-five kilos."

Even while disbelieving that it could actually happen to them, her family was ghettoized within the city. They received special treatment because of her grandfather's status in the community, and Alice created ways of working around the rules to accomplish her goals. In fact, she found many ways of escaping from the ghetto to move within the community at large, perhaps because she was a child. Her father managed to escape and gained assistance and protection in Budapest from Raoul Wallenberg.

Alice remembered the transport with her mother and siblings from the ghetto to the railroad station. "Marching through our town was like a scene out of the Bible. . . . I could not tell you the humiliation I felt; carrying our baggage, passing our house, looking into our window, seeing the people who occupied our house looking at us, and nobody stopping." The Jews were shocked that the townspeople were uncaring bystanders to this cruel injustice. Cattle cars transported the Jews to Auschwitz in 1944.

Alice described how people were sorted into the lines of life and death and how she was separated from her mother and young brothers who were immediately sent to the gas chambers. Her sister Edith was separated and sent into another line, and Alice was unsure of her fate. "Seconds . . . everything, seconds. It was like . . . like in a mirage because first your eyes were not even used to the light after this darkness in the cattle train; and then this sunlight . . . this strong sunlight and the shouting. . . . And I step aside, realizing in a few minutes that I don't see Mother. I don't see my brothers. I don't see Edith. I'm totally alone."

At the age of fifteen, Alice was introduced to Auschwitz. Her principal goal was to find her sister Edith. Upon discovering that Edith was still alive, Alice resolved to be with her. Through creative efforts, a note was passed to Edith, housed within another Lager (camp) barrack. In the weeks that followed, Edith and another prisoner exchanged barrack positions during the transport of food to the opposite Lager, and the two sisters were brought back together. "And so Edith and I were reunited in Auschwitz. It was such a miracle. I just knew that I never wanted to be without her ever, ever. And we clung to each other; but it was very risky because there started to be selections."

The sisters created many plans and deceptions as a means of staying together, while constantly protecting each other. During Edith's hospitalization for high fever, Alice manipulated her environment to visit Edith in the infirmary. Alice gained access by being willing to do unpleasant jobs, such as carrying dead people from the barracks. To bring hope to her sister and other patients, Alice made up stories that told of saviors on their way. Her goal was to create hope for her ailing sister and all the others in the hospital, thereby increasing their resiliency and likelihood of survival.

Edith recuperated and returned to the barrack, but very quickly the Blockälteste (prisoner in charge of the barrack) selected a group of children for liquidation. The Blockälteste told them they would receive warm clothes, so the girls filed into the showers to get disinfected and receive new clothes. "But it turned out that the shower did not work, that it was really the gas chamber. And the tragic . . . the realization came only after we came back, and this Blockälteste couldn't believe that we are alive. She looked at us and she started to scream, 'How could it happen? Why are you back? You're not supposed to be back.' I think that was one of the rare times in Auschwitz that the gas did not work."

At the time of another selection in Auschwitz, the sisters were selected to go together to Guben, a subcamp of Gross-Rosen. Once again, by manipulating their environment, the two sisters manufactured a means of staying together and were transported to labor in an ammunition factory. Though the sisters were placed in a children's barrack, the subcamp labor was extremely strenuous and difficult.

In February 1945 the camp was forced on a death march, during which Alice, her sister Edith and a friend escaped from the group by hiding in a hay pile. Some townspeople discovered them and sent all three to the police station, despite their pleading. The trio devised a story, saying that they had mistakenly overslept and did not know that the group was leaving the area. The police sentenced them to be shot, but they escaped again by creating a story that got them into a cattle car that was departing. Once again they escaped the grips of death, though they were sent to Bergen-Belsen.

"Nothing ever in literature could compare to anything that Bergen-Belsen was. When we arrived, the dead were no longer carried away anymore. You stepped over them. You fell over them if you couldn't walk. There were people in agony, begging for water . . . it was hell."

At the time of liberation, Alice and her sister feared being separated because Edith was violently ill. To remain with her sister, Alice pretended she also was sick. After being separated from her sister by the liberators, Alice never saw her sister again. She struggled constantly to find Edith and was sent to Sweden with hope of finding her there, to no avail. Alice was contacted in Sweden with the news that her father was alive. With the help of rescuers, she eventually reunited with him. To this day, she has never learned what happened to her sister Edith and presumes she perished after liberation.

In 1946 Alice returned to Budapest, and in 1948 she emigrated to Israel on *The Exodus.* She studied at Taipiot Teacher's College in Tel Aviv and pursued art training. In Israel she met and married her husband and later moved to the United States. Her husband became a rabbi, as did their two sons. They also gave birth to a daughter with Down's syndrome, who Alice felt was a gift from G–d.

In 1978 Alice returned to Hungary and discovered no memorials had been constructed in honor of Hungarian Jews. She was devastated, knowing that it was "almost as if we never existed." She also found no further traces of her family members.

After her visit to Hungary, Alice began creating artworks to memorialize the Holocaust. Her artwork incorporated mixed media with photos, newspaper clippings, documents and paint, and have been exhibited in the Hebrew Union Skirball Cultural Center in Los Angeles, the United States House of Representatives, Yad Vashem, the Holocaust Memorial Museum Houston and the United States Holocaust Memorial Museum in

Washington, D.C. Lehigh University recently displayed her artwork when she spoke about the presentation of the Holocaust through art.

Alice currently lives in Texas with her family and is active with the United States Holocaust Memorial Museum.

HOW ALICE C. COPED

Alice and her sister clearly exhibited both emotion-focused coping, through affiliation and supporting each other through words of hope and compassion, and problem-focused coping to manipulate their environment. Alice used problem-focused coping to protect her sister and herself and was very appreciative of assistance from others. By constantly looking for ways to remain together and to escape the inevitable, the sisters avoided the grip of death on many occasions. The sisters promised after their first day in Auschwitz that they would never be separated again and created all sorts of strategies to manipulate the environment. Creating stories, such as the one used to hide in the cattle car after their escape from the death march and capture, the two girls were able to adapt to the situation and within minutes find options for their safety. In terms of emotion-based coping, the affiliation between the two sisters was so strong that it was the primary source of adaptation and coping for survival. While constantly surveying the environment, the two formed a bond that was their primary means for survival.

Through the Eyes of Alice C.

Everybody can choose what they want to do in life with themselves, go right or go left. And the Torah says, 'Choose life.' But the important thing is what life you're choosing. Not only the self-gratification, not only the self. But choose life. Look at the life of the others, and help and stand up where . . . where unrighteousness and evil (are) done. And stand up and be counted. We all have the ability, just like Raoul Wallenberg. This (video) tape is (not only) for my grandchildren but for all the grandchildren, for all the children I will not meet. If they're looking for heroes, they have to look into their souls and find the hero in themselves.

4

Nina K.
Love's Advantage

ina K. was born on April 11, 1929, in Grodno in the northeastern corner of Poland. Her family of four lived in a beautiful apartment near the River Niemen. Nina, her sister, Sala, and her parents were active within the community at large of their small town, where her father was a forester. Nina's sister was a champion skater and swimmer, and Nina was a soloist musician who was also interested in theater. Educated in Jewish and Catholic schools within Poland, the children viewed their childhood as a "free, delightful existence" filled with love and lots of attention.

Nina recollected that there was anti-Semitism, but she was not targeted because she was blue-eyed and blonde. She said that in 1938 and 1939, with the rise in anti-Semitism, some rocks were thrown at her family's apartment windows, including during Passover. Her father was imprisoned for three or four months for political reasons by the Communists, who ruled the traditional northeastern part of Poland.

In September 1941 the Nazis occupied Grodno. "I was playing with dolls one day, and the next day I was asked to be a grown-up. It hadn't quite sunk in, what the tragedy of the entire period meant. . . . I was in a vacuum."

Shortly after the occupation, the Nazis established two ghettos in Grodno. The upper ghetto became home for Nina and her family as they were uprooted, as was the entire Jewish community. On one occasion, some peasant families suggested to Nina's father that the two children could be hidden with Polish families because they did not look Jewish. Nina remembered that she and her sister had a discussion in which they decided they did not want to be separated from their parents.

Nina said that life in the ghetto was bearable because she was with her family. She and Sala played and improvised. In 1942

Nina and her sister were separated from their parents, who were taken to Auschwitz. The two girls remained in the ghetto and worked in a tobacco factory. They were able to escape several selections. "We continued to give ourselves some kind of moral support by saying, 'Look, we'll probably leave here and I'm sure we'll be with our parents again.'"

On January 20, 1943, the ghetto was liquidated and Sala put her mother's coat on Nina to make her appear much older and stronger. "It was a long coat, and I think that coat may have been responsible for my going into the camp rather than to the crematory right away. My sister was very bright. She was very clever." Sala instructed Nina not to say a word, then watched the selection process and told Nina to walk over to a small group of people who were being separated from the larger mass. "There were eighty-five women and a hundred and twenty men out of something like twenty-five hundred who were then brought into Auschwitz. The rest went directly to the gas chambers." The two girls entered Auschwitz, with two thousand others from the Grodno ghetto, on January 24, 1943, with the smell of flesh burning and the chimneys bellowing with smoke and fire. Nina was tattooed with the number 31386 and her sister with 31387. They were shaved and taken to a block within the camp. "It was rather painful, and my sister, knowing the fear I had for doctors, whispered for me to have courage. A triangle was tattooed underneath the number."

Nina described her first months in Auschwitz: "These were probably the most horrendously difficult months, the first three months. If you survived the first day, maybe you survived a second. If you made it through a week, chances are you might make it to the second week. Time had no meaning. . . . Usually someone died during the night. We were all assigned sooner or later to carry dead bodies from the barracks to the outside wall. I washed my hands with the tears that were flowing freely from my eyes."

After those three months, Sala became very ill. Nina pleaded with her sister, who had never been sick a day in her life, to keep moving. "It was a Friday, and I said 'I don't care whether you can get up—you've got to get up, because if you don't, they will take you to Block 25 (hospital).'" Because she was unable to rise, Sala was taken to Block 25. The diagnosis was typhoid. Nina visited Sala in the hospital. On Sunday, April 10, Sala died in Nina's arms. "I cried bitterly that day, and then I did not cry for years and years. I became very unfeeling, very strong inside. . . . Watching this incredible drama was a woman I did not know. She . . . came up to me and said in German, which I did not understand very well then, she said, 'I don't have any children. I'm not married. But if I had a little girl, I would like her to look just like you and be just like you.'" The woman, named Martha, was a Jewish prisoner and nurse who cared for Nina for the remainder of their stay in Auschwitz. Martha was about twenty years older than Nina. "She saved my life about four or five times. Four from the gas chambers and others when I was deathly ill with typhoid, or God knows what else. She would steal injections and save me that way."

Humanity was not lost among the inmates. Nina remembered, "People did care for each other. People did give each other moral support. People did commiserate with each other and tried to help. There was very little because people were dying and the suffering was so intense that it was very difficult to give strength to someone else, but Martha is a perfect example."

There were no hospitals, and Jews who were sent to Block 25 generally did not return. On one occasion, Martha was able to smuggle Nina into a Christian hospital, perhaps because she did not look Jewish. Though Dr. Kliner targeted Nina during a selection for death, Martha told Nina that her name had been "miraculously" erased from Kliner's list and that she would not be exterminated in the gas chamber on that day.

Nina was transferred to Lager C and met Irma Grese, the head female SS guard in Auschwitz. Meeting her was absolutely terrifying for Nina. Grese always had a German shepherd and a whip, which she used very freely. One day, Nina entered the Lager and saw Grese standing there in civilian clothes. Nina remembered Grese as a vision to behold. "She took my little cheek and she said, 'They tell me that you look a lot like me, and I wanted to be sure that was really true.' And I, in my total naiveness, said, 'Oh, I don't think there's any . . . I've never seen anyone more beautiful,' and I meant it. I mean she was like a vision." Grese, who had total power to do anything she wished at any time to anyone, took a liking to Nina and assigned her to be a lookout standing guard in front of the barrack, while she raped the most beautiful Jewish women. Nina was given extra food for her job. "Grese would make us stand for Appells for hours in the freezing weather. People would faint. She would trod on them. She would beat them. She would sic her dog (on them)."

Nina stated that Auschwitz was created for one purpose: the liquidation of Jews and other undesirables. She also declared that, as part of this mission, Grese and Commandant Kramer were chosen because of their predisposition to evil, because they were a "different breed of people." "They looked human, but these were not human beings. They . . . people, humanity as we know it, even in the worst possible way, cannot behave that way."

Nina remained in Auschwitz for two years. Her survival there is a two-fold oddity because there were relatively no children in Auschwitz and because very few people could withstand two years of atrocities and horrors in the depths of Auschwitz.

Nina was evacuated from the camp on January 18, 1945, and was sent to Ravensbruck, a camp built for three thousand and housing twenty thousand. Nina stayed in Ravensbruck for three weeks, during which time she met up with Martha. Nina said that the camp was filled with "masses of people, death, terrible starvation, no work." When separated from Martha again, Nina gave up her desire to live and was sent to Retzow-am-Rechlin, which was not originally a concentration-camp location and has been described as a relatively nice camp. There Nina was designated as a "Lauferin," a gofer for anyone who needed her assistance.

A nineteen-year-old German soldier named Lucien took a liking to Nina at Retzow-am-Rechlin. Nina discovered during some conversations that he was a medical student from Luxembourg. He claimed to have no knowledge of the brutality that had occurred. He was determined to protect Nina, so he created a scheme to smuggle her out of the concentration camp. He said he was willing to risk his life for her. Lucien contacted a woman in the nearby village and told Nina, "I will take you there when there is a break. I promise you." "And I asked him, 'Why are you doing it?' He said, 'Because I love you.' Now you have to understand that here was a Jewish girl, sixteen years old, speaking to a German, to a man wearing a German uniform who was saying 'I love you and I'm not going to let you die. I'm going to help you.'" Lucien predicted the evacuation on May 5, 1945, and kept his promise of smuggling Nina to safety. Later he was sent to the Russian front, where it was reported he died.

Knowing that no family of hers was left in Grodno, Nina went to Prague, where Martha found her. The American Joint Distribution Committee brought Nina to London, where she lived for four years and began her musical studies, first in piano, then in voice. She continued these studies and later made her professional debut with the City Symphony of New York.

In 1950, at the age of twenty-one, Nina emigrated to the United States. She sailed to New York on the *Queen Elizabeth* and reunited with an aunt who had emigrated to the United States in 1921 with Nina's grandmother. She performed with the Philadelphia Grand Opera Company and the Washington Opera Society. In 1963 she won the Concert Artist's Guild Award and gave a recital in New York's Town Hall. She has sung with the New Jersey Symphony Orchestra, Washington Opera Society, and the Philadelphia Grand Opera Company and has presented numerous recitals at Carnegie Recital Hall. She continued giving private voice lessons in Philadelphia and had her last public concert in 1974 at the Walnut Street Theatre.

In 1979, Cornell University's Sage Chapel, the oldest inter-denominational chapel in academia in the United States, invited Nina to campus for three days to address the students and faculty and to make a Sunday presentation that was broadcast live throughout the Ithaca-Syracuse area. At the time, Nina had only a fifth-grade education.

Nina has had two children and two grandchildren. In 1980, when her sons were getting their master's degrees, Nina followed them into academia. She graduated cum laude with an associate degree from the University of Pennsylvania and earned a master's degree in rhetoric and communication from Temple University.

In 1994 Nina received the Creative Excellence Award from the International Foundation of Employee Benefit Plans for her groundbreaking work in the field of employee benefits.

Nina is deeply committed to working for better Jewish-Christian understanding and human rights.

HOW NINA K. COPED

Nina reported that you could not let your defenses down if you wanted to survive in Auschwitz. "It is not a question of strength. You don't ever know what's happening to you. It is a sort of self . . . self-discipline by saying, 'If I'm going to make it, I'm going to retreat from all that and emerge in a way into my own fantasy world.'" Nina created a world that converged within the emotion-focused coping mechanism she utilized to survive. She reported that she used humor, which has always been central to the heart of Jewish experience, on numerous occasions. She believed that if you did not have a sense of humor, you would die from experiencing all that occurred in Auschwitz. Nina tells people she has "a Ph.D. from Auschwitz. That covers a lot of ground, doesn't it?"

The fact that Nina survived in Auschwitz for two years, especially as a child, is perhaps partially due to being protected by Martha and Lucien, and even Irma Grese. Nina believed, and still does, that Martha's protection and affiliation were the most essential forces for her survival.

Nina reported that she could not account for other factors that helped her survive and that she is still uncertain why she survived Auschwitz. "Maybe there is some plan that the heavens, God, whatever, that I'm here. Maybe to bear witness. . . . I don't think I could function as a human being and be as accomplished in many ways and continue on with my life if I had to live and remember what happened to me there. And I think again here the mind works some miracles."

PHONE INTERVIEW WITH NINA K.

Nina stated that problem-focused coping was impossible for her because there were no choices, no ways to manipulate her environment. She reported that in Auschwitz one had no control whatsoever in one's life. There were no coping strategies that were active in nature. "I have a predisposition to being an optimist —you survive the day . . . hour to hour. . . . If you live for one day in Auschwitz, then perhaps for another day, for two days."

You didn't "feel like you had any choices . . . you were thrown into whatever." Nina believed that luck, fate, and "a hope, a dream, and fantasy" played a part in her survival, but in her opinion they were not active techniques that were consciously used for survival purposes. Nina emphasized that she used the emotion-focused coping mechanism of fantasy in her efforts to survive. "Pain emerges and you go into another world of fantasy. With despair you go into fantasy. It is amazing how your mind regenerates itself."

Nina believed that her affiliation with Martha was a dominant force in her survival. "She was very instrumental . . . she took care of me . . . she hid me . . . gave me injections to save my life." Nina believed being very young, trusting and naive also may have aided in her survival.

Through the Eyes of Nina K.

I don't think I could function as a human being and be as accomplished in many ways and continue with my life if I had to live and remember what happened to me there. And I think . . . the mind works some miracles . . . you remember what is essential, but you sort of forget all the other—it is like having a baby—you remember the beauty but you don't remember the pain because otherwise no woman would ever have a baby. And Auschwitz was . . . the cradle of death. It gave people who were deranged the absolute opportunity to exercise their wildest macabre behavior.

The Holocaust . . . is not a Jewish issue. It is a universal issue that affects each and every one of us, and the more the American public, the European people, anyone . . . understands the historical, the sociological, the philosophical aspects of the Holocaust, the better off we all are because this is the greatest lesson that we can learn about humanity in any form or shape that you want. . . . History has an ugly way of repeating itself and we cannot allow that to happen.

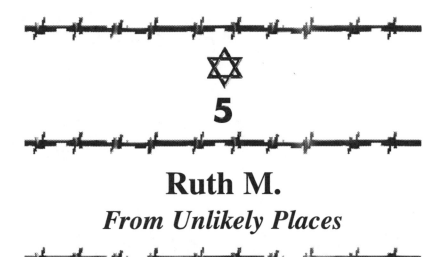

Ruth M.
From Unlikely Places

uth M. was born on June 23, 1929, in Frankfurt, Germany. She and her younger brother lived with their parents in the city, where their father was in the leather-goods business. In 1933 the country was undergoing a political and anti-Semitic upheaval, and fear was rampant. Each time her parents left home, Ruth was certain something would happen to them and that they would not return to her safely. Ruth's uncle was a journalist who was "hunted down" because of his political views. Reports say he was captured in Czechoslovakia, placed in jail and executed.

Changes within the country included the discontinuation of economic transactions in Jewish banks, beatings and harassment of Jews, restrictions on Jewish education, a prohibition against listening to Jewish composers, seizure of Jewish businesses, and discontinuation of protection and civil liberties for Jewish citizens.

One of Ruth's earliest memories of the Nazi police state in the early 1930s was an incident involving a friend's father who was disliked by the Nazis. To punish him, they took his eight-year-old daughter and had her sterilized.

During the early years of the Nazi regime, the Germans transported many Jews out of Germany. Ruth's father had a choice of staying in Germany to run his business, which had been taken over by a Nazi, or of being sent to the east, and he chose to stay behind with his family to protect them from harm. Ruth's family was one of the last families of "full Jews" sent to Auschwitz with Polish prisoners in April 1943. Ruth remembered that "off-springs"—half-Jews (Mischlinge)—were sent to Theresienstadt, while her family was sent on a transport to Auschwitz. The transport carried only thirty-seven Jews, plus non-Jewish prisoners. "We were taken away on the nineteenth of April, which was

Hitler's birthday or the twentieth or something, it was . . .
supposed to be a birthday present to the Führer, that Germany
would be Judenrein (Jewish free), and that was why they . . .
shipped . . . gathered us on the nineteenth of April, and . . . it took
us about a week to get there."

Upon arrival, Ruth, her nine-year-old brother and her mother
were taken to the women's camp. At age thirteen, Ruth saw her
father for the last time. Ruth expressed the humiliation and fear
she felt while standing in the nude and being tattooed and shaved
of all body hair.

To demoralize them and strip them of their strength, honor and
Jewish identities, the women were forced to make road repairs
within the camp. "They were interested in having people get sick
and having people . . . die or be in such condition that they would
take them to the gas chambers."

Ruth contracted typhus, and her mother protected her during
the workday. Once, during a selection, Ruth was placed in the
line for extermination. "My mother pleaded with him (SS) and
said . . . well, she's my child, and she, can't she come with, can't
I come with her and he said, 'No, but if you're so concerned
about your daughter, go with her' . . . and one of the women who
was working in the barrack . . . but she had some kind of . . . protected position whatever that was worth . . . she sort of grabbed
me under one arm and my mother grabbed my other arm, and we
managed to walk away." Ruth and her mother proceeded into the
general group without being noticed. To this day Ruth is unsure
if the SS guard pretended not to notice that she had slipped into
the group saved from extermination.

Ruth remembered that on another occasion a German soldier
hid her brother and mother behind a pile of coal to protect her
brother from selection and extermination. When asked why he

rescued them, the soldier told Ruth's mother that he had witnessed a mass shooting in a village and a woman forced to choose between her children. Faced with a "choiceless choice" of which child would live and which would die, the woman had grabbed both children and jumped into the mass grave. The German guard had sworn after witnessing the atrocity that if he could "ever save a mother and a child, he would make it his mission to do so. And he did that by saving my mother and my brother and hiding them for the day. . . . I never knew who the man was . . . it was just a very strange and humane gesture in a . . . sea or in . . . a surrounding of inhumanity." Later, Ruth recalled, "they decided that it wasn't moral for a young boy to live with all these women . . . and my brother was taken to the men's camp, and he managed to live through it somehow."

Ruth faced punishment when she bridged the language gap by speaking English to two young Greek girls. She reported that speaking English was forbidden. One of the girls, Nina, an opera singer, sang many times for the prisoners. On one occasion, an SS officer asked the girl to move into his house to sing for him. She refused the offer, despite the fact that it might mean an easier life and that the sacrifice was tremendous. "She refused him. And . . . among the next . . . selections to the gas chamber, her number was prominently mentioned and there was no way that anyone could have erased the number. I mean he made sure that she was on that next transport to the gas chamber." Ruth noted that this was one of the "real unforgettable friendships" she formed within the concentration camp.

Ruth was assigned to work in Kanada, which was the sorting center for all belongings taken from prisoners brought into the camp. Clothes, which were in good condition, were sorted and shipped back to the Reich for use by German citizens. Ruth remembered that she stole a belt from Kanada. This act of resistance helped her keep her dress off the ground when she was forced to walk through the mud, which caked on her clothes and physically weighed her down. Ruth kept the belt as a reminder after her liberation from Auschwitz.

Ruth remembered her mother risking her own life for a woman who had lost her children. Ruth's mother ran through a multitude of bullets from the watchtower guards and heroically pulled away the woman, who was determined to commit suicide on the electrified wire fence.

On November 1, 1944, guards placed Ruth and her mother on a transport to Ravensbruck and the subcamp of Malchow. The prisoners were forced to make bullets and hand grenades in an ammunition factory for the German army. Ruth reported that she tried on numerous occasions to "sort of squeeze them in a crooked way (bullets) so that they would close, but not quite, and I was hoping that these bullets would misfire and I was hoping that in this way it would be my part of the war effort against the Nazis."

Ruth and her mother were liberated from the Malchow camp during a forced death march in May 1945. They returned to Frankfurt to find any remaining family. They later emigrated to America, where Ruth met and married an American soldier. The soldier's mother felt her son had married beneath him because Ruth was European and had been in a concentration camp. That, Ruth said, was the common attitude of Americans, Jews and others: Those who had been in the camps were lowly and despicable.

For twenty years Ruth did not speak of her experiences, as if it were a badge of shame. "But, I think we as survivors . . . as prisoners of the Nazis were told that we were subhumans . . . and

I think it was drilled into us that we kept actually believing that it still was true. We really should have had lots of counseling."

Life was quite difficult for survivors. Ruth and others had no real support system, no family, and their backgrounds had been destroyed by the Nazis. They felt lost in a foreign environment that didn't seem to open their arms to them.

Upon reflection fifty years later, Ruth stated it was essential that she continued to speak about the Holocaust so others could be informed about what really had happened. "Perhaps it can be a warning to the people, to the world. We are trying in our little way . . . we as the survivors . . . are trying to say this is what happened. Beware! Don't fall into this sort of inhumanity (ever again)."

HOW RUTH M. COPED

Ruth's testimony is filled with examples of emotion-focused coping related to affiliation and protection from others, such as her mother fighting for Ruth's survival, as well as for the survival of other women in the camp. Ruth's affiliation with friends also was evident in her coping, and she noted that her relationship with Nini, the young girl who sang opera, was a "real unforgettable friendship" from the time she was captive in Auschwitz until she was taken away.

Ruth's testimony recollected numerous examples of those who reached out to assist others during the massive traumatization. Her mother saving the woman who was suicidal illustrates this point. The poignant example of the SS guard who saved Ruth's mother and her brother from extermination is another amazing example of affiliation and protection of others, despite the fact that the assistance came from a German SS guard who risked his life to save Jews.

Ruth spoke of a pregnant woman who hid her condition and was protected by other women risking their lives to conceal the pregnancy and maintain the woman's survival. This act of concealment is another remarkable example of group affiliation. Ruth stated the woman had a child on Christmas day. She and other women believed that this was a sign that a miracle would happen and that, if they all held on long enough, one day they would all be liberated.

Ruth's testimony illustrated some problem-focused coping via acts of resistance and defiance, such as in her choice to speak to other girls in English, which was forbidden in the camp. Other acts of resistance included Ruth's stealing of the belt when she worked in Kanada, as well as putting the bullets together in the ammunition factory in Malchow in such a way that they might misfire.

Helen G.
The Bonds of Sisterhood

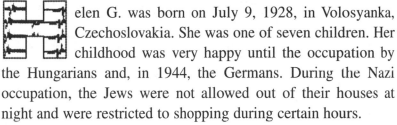 elen G. was born on July 9, 1928, in Volosyanka, Czechoslovakia. She was one of seven children. Her childhood was very happy until the occupation by the Hungarians and, in 1944, the Germans. During the Nazi occupation, the Jews were not allowed out of their houses at night and were restricted to shopping during certain hours.

After six weeks of Nazi occupation, all Jews were rounded up and taken to a ghetto in Uzhgorod, in the capital of Carpathia. Two weeks before the ghettoization, the Nazis transported Helen's brothers and father to a work camp. Helen's grandparents, sister and mother remained in the ghetto. Her grandfather, eighty years old, took his Torah to the ghetto, and one day all the older Jews who had beards were told to report to a certain barrack. "They made these men put on their *talleisim,* their prayer shawls, and they told them to start praying. And while they were praying, they started beating them and cutting their beards. . . . So this poor old man had to endure the pain, not only the physical pain, the beatings, but also the blasphemous cutting of the beard."

After six weeks the ghetto was liquidated. Helen was sent to Auschwitz with her family. They were packed into a cattle car with only a small window on the top. Helen climbed on her sister's shoulders to look out the window and witnessed a horrifying sight. "I saw farmers showing to me like this (fingers across throat). I . . . I really didn't know what they were saying. And . . . it just didn't sink into my head that they're telling me something. . . . I told my sister. I told my mother that's what they were showing me. Well, anyway, until we got to Auschwitz, it sort of didn't sink in."

Helen's family was separated upon arrival. Helen's brother was ripped from his mother's arms, and she went running and screaming after her son until she was beaten by the guards. Helen's mother pleaded to have her six-year-old child returned. Many of the mothers put up a fight to keep their children and were beaten, while the young children were grabbed and thrown haphazardly into trucks. The guards beat Helen's mother and pushed her into the line to the left. Helen and her sister were the only two family members sent to the right, to the line of life. There were so many people walking toward the showers that the Nazis could not burn them fast enough in the crematorium, so they burned them in huge pits.

"There was a man telling us that they are burning people in pits because they can't burn them in the ovens. They can burn more than they can gas. And then we hear music! It was very, very confusing to us." Their captors forced Helen and her sister into a large room to undress. Many of the girls put their heads down, and the SS pulled up the women's heads and beat them with their whips. Shaved of all hair and dignity that night, they were then placed into a barrack.

Helen looked through the cracks of the barrack the next morning. "I saw people hanging on these wire fences. It was such a terrible sight. . . . They were electrocuted because many of them . . . some of them were aware of the electric fences and some of them thought maybe they want to escape or to go look for their parents or go look for their family. So they . . . they were hanging there." During that first day Helen was beaten by a Kapo until she was black and blue because, she was told, she took too long to go to the bathroom.

During a special selection after five weeks in Auschwitz, anyone who appeared strong enough was taken into a separate line. Helen and her sister were put into another barrack and taken out of Auschwitz. "We felt we were going to get out of this place, because, as you know, I mean . . . getting out from Auschwitz by a gate and not by chimney . . . I was lucky." Helen, her sister and approximately one thousand other girls were transported by cattle car to work in a German ammunition plant. The Allies bombed the ammunition factory every night, and Helen prayed they would be hit.

The gunpowder in the work camp poisoned the girls. Their eyes became yellow, as did their bodies, and their hair grew in red. Many of the girls died due to poor ventilation from the toxic materials within the factory.

After working in the ammunition plant for a few months, Helen told her sister she could live no longer. "I just felt mentally I can't go on any more." Helen's sister supported her and screamed, "'You're not gonna leave me here alone. You're not gonna die.' So I was trying to hold on to my life because I saw that she cared . . . you know, the way she carried on." Pushed to stay alive, Helen and her sister continued to work as the numbers of girls dwindled to five hundred and eventually to fewer than two hundred.

Helen said the girls attempted to help each other, but all of them were experiencing loss of strength and hope while trying desperately to survive. Helen's sister held her up during Appells on numerous occasions and literally dragged her to work while she did her work in addition to Helen's. "We didn't look like people . . . we were a different color . . . we were yellow and we had orange-red hair. I weighed maybe seventy or sixty pounds and was burned up with the gunpowder."

Approximately nine months later, the Allies bombed the ammunition factory. Nevertheless, the Nazis took the remaining two hundred women outside to build a road. They were then transported to Bergen-Belsen, which by then had become a mountain of dead corpses. Within a month, Helen's sister contracted typhus and became delirious with fever. "She was the strong one. I was the sick one and she got sick." Soon after this, in May 1945, the Allies liberated the camp and took Helen's sister to a hospital.

Helen was unsure if her sister had survived, and she searched through the dead corpses, trying to find her. After a week or so, Helen heard that her sister had survived and they reunited, remaining in a hospital at Bergen-Belsen until they felt stronger. They were then transported to a hospital in Sweden.

Eventually they reunited with an older sister in Brooklyn, where Helen soon married and had three children and, ultimately, nine grandchildren.

Helen experienced post-traumatic stress disorder and remembered how she suffered with constant nightmares and despair. "I recognized that we were alone . . . we already figured out what happened to our family . . . to tell you the truth, we didn't allow ourselves to think that they would take all the kids that came with us to the gas chamber . . . our mother, our grandfather, our grandmother and the family that came with us . . . who went to the gas chamber to be gassed for no sins committed."

Helen reported that she had lost all of her family except for her sister. "I couldn't talk about it for a long time. . . . But sometimes I would just go in and cry for weeks. . . . I know I cannot bring my family back, my little brother, the million and a half children who were destroyed, who were gassed, but perhaps maybe I could reach some people and make them understand that this did happen and it can happen again if we are not going to be . . . if we are not going to be aware of our surroundings."

Helen now speaks frequently about the Holocaust and devotes herself to teaching children the lessons of the Holocaust.

HOW HELEN G. COPED

The way Helen affiliated with her sister is a prime example of the powerful motivation to survive through emotion-focused coping. Determined to live and support each other, the two faced each day in an effort to survive. Helen reported that her sister was a very powerful influence, that she encouraged Helen to live despite the fact that many times she wanted to give up. Helen was also a very powerful factor in her sister's survival during internment.

Helen reported that a person wants to survive, to have a purpose or a will to live. The relationship between the two sisters motivated them to survive the atrocities that surrounded their internment in Auschwitz, working camps and Bergen-Belsen. Helen also said that her survival involved luck and chance and that denial played a vital part in her coping and adaptation during internment.

Through the Eyes of Helen G.

I know I cannot bring back my family, my little brother, the million and a half children who were destroyed, who were gassed, but perhaps maybe, I could reach some people (and) make them understand that this did happen and it can happen again if we are not going to be aware of our surroundings. I think that every person . . . every person on earth should examine this, what happened in the Holocaust, because a thing like that can happen again, and we need to watch that it shouldn't ever happen again to any minority.

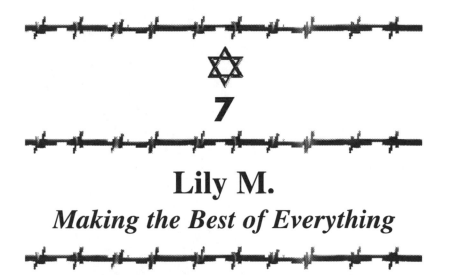

Lily M.
Making the Best of Everything

ily M. was born in 1928 in Antwerp, Belgium. Her father left his family and emigrated to the United States just months before Lily was born. Lily's early childhood memories include being separated from her older brother and sister when her mother experienced difficulty raising three children alone while continuing to work. Lily's mother took care of Lily's older sister and brother in Brussels, and Lily's grandmother raised her in a Jewish neighborhood in Antwerp.

Lily heard rumors as a child about Hitler's treatment of Jews in Poland. Her grandmother proclaimed that she would rather die than live through another pogrom like the ones she had endured in Poland. In 1939 Lily's grandmother died of cancer, and in 1940, after Lily had lived with her mother in Brussels for one year, the Nazis invaded Belgium. Rising anti-Semitism and the targeting of Jews slowly affected the Jewish population by way of various edicts legislated within the city. Unsure of Belgian reaction, the German Reich moved slowly with its new laws, first requiring a curfew for Jews and later the wearing of the yellow star. The Germans collected passports belonging to Jews and required Jews to register with the governmental bodies of Brussels. Jews were offered jobs in nearby towns, but those who volunteered for work were never heard from again.

By 1942 the Germans began raiding neighborhoods and collecting and transporting Jews to ghettos and transit camps. During Lily's hospitalization for tonsillitis, a friend of Lily's mother offered to hide Lily's older sister Marja with a family in the country. Upon resisting sexual relations arranged by her "rescuer," Lily's sister was denounced and transported to a transit camp.

"When she was . . . taken out of . . . Belgium to . . . the camp, she had slipped a postal card through . . . through the cracks of the cattle wagon. And . . . early in the morning as people were going to work and the farmers were going to work in their fields, they would pick up notes and cards that people dropped from the . . . wagons. And . . . this is how we got our card from my sister, saying, 'Beware of this woman because she took me to this man who wanted to have relationships with me. And I wouldn't give in, and I got denounced.'"

After that incident, the same woman denounced Lily's mother and brother. Lily was warned after her tonsillectomy that she should stay with her aunt for protection on the outskirts of Brussels. She remained in hiding with her aunt and uncle until 1944. The Nazis were discovering Jews throughout the area, and Gentiles who knew Lily suggested she change her name to appear non-Jewish. "Lily, let's call you Lilliane from now on. . . . Nobody will know that you are Jewish." Upon that recommendation, Lily hid her identity and worked in a little factory doing part-time work and in a beauty parlor.

"As the years . . . 1940 to 1944, at the end it was getting real tough on us. And . . . as we were struggling to survive, one day I came home from work and the people downstairs told us that we have to get out." New Gentile tenants in the buildings denounced them, and the following day the German soldiers came to arrest Lily, her aunt and her uncle. Fortunately, they had been warned in advance and hidden by other Gentile rescuers.

Lily remained hidden in safety by a friend and separated from her aunt and uncle until she visited them two weeks later and was captured by the SS. Lily and her family were gathered with other captured Jews and placed in Malines (Mechelen, in German), a small town between Brussels and Antwerp. Lily and her family remained in this transit detention camp for approximately six weeks until enough "undesirables" were gathered for transport.

"I was in the twenty-fifth transport that left Malines. And after that, there was one more transport; and then Belgium was liberated."

She was taken with others by cattle car to Birkenau, where those on the transport were divided into lines sent to the "right or to the left. . . . And at that time I did not know what that meant. And he (Mengele) told me to go to the right, and he told my aunt to go to the left. . . . But I never saw her after that again. . . . I was fifteen years old, and I was all alone in this hell. . . . They tattooed me; and they told us from now on, this is my name. My name is A-5143. . . . This was the second time. The first time, they made a mistake with the whole transport. So they called us back and they scratched the first number out, and then they gave us the second number. . . . And the delusion, the disappointment, the discouragement that I felt. I felt like I was not a human person anymore. They had shaved our heads; I felt so ashamed. And also when they told us to undress and to shower, they made us feel like—like we were animals. The men were walking around and laughing and looking at us. And you take a young girl at the age, who had never been exposed to . . . a person . . . to a man, and you stay there naked. . . . I wanted the ground should open, and I should go in it."

Unable to make sense of the inhumanity, the atrocities and the evil, Lily decided to make the "best out of everything . . . to survive in the jungle." She forced herself to eat and maintained her hope of surviving to return to her remaining aunt in Belgium. During her six weeks in Birkenau, Lily volunteered with a group of other young girls from Belgium for a work detail.

"We had made a pact that we should stick together, because our parents had been taken together into the gas chambers." The group of twenty-five or thirty Belgian girls were taken to

Auschwitz to work in the kitchen in a new Lager (Zwei-B Lager). Lily remained in the kitchen for six months. She smuggled food one night during that time to Hungarian transports who had not been fed. Though caught by the Blockälteste, Lily was sent not to her death but to her barrack. She discovered the next day that the entire transport had been liquidated. "They were all gone. And I could have lost my life. I didn't realize what I was doing. But I felt in my heart that I wanted to help these people, and this is all I could do."

Lily was helped by her friends after being badly scalded by boiling coffee, and she believed her affiliation with other girls helped her escape the grips of Dr. Mengele's selection. She reported that many Jews gave up, and others threw themselves against the electrified wire fences, but she would sneak behind the barracks and look at the night sky. "And I would see the sky. . . . I would see the stars. And I would talk to myself; and I would say, 'I can't believe that these stars are looking down at us in this hell in this camp, and the same stars are shining at the outside world. And other people are looking at the same stars, and they are free. And they are free to do what they want to do. And they are living a good life. And we are here in hell—human beings worse than animals.'" After a long cry, Lily would return to the barrack and face the next morning's Appell.

Upon learning that Belgium had been liberated, Lily regained hope that she would eventually return to her remaining aunt in Belgium. As Russian soldiers approached, Auschwitz prisoners were sent on a forced death march. "I don't know how many days we walked. We walked, and then we took cattle cars, and then we walked again. . . . We saw people lying all over: on top of hills, behind trees . . . it was really like a war zone. And this is how we finally arrived in a camp called Bergen-Belsen." Lily found dehumanizing conditions and complete lack of showers and sanitary facilities. "In Auschwitz at least we worked. And . . . we were afraid to go to the showers because we didn't know if it would give us water or gas. We had no toilets. The decay and filth in Bergen-Belsen were indescribable."

Within the camp, Lily protected a young French girl named Christiane, who became a meaning or purpose to survive. Christiane was infected with typhus and began screaming out of control one day. Lily tried to feed and calm her, but the child died in her arms. Christiane's body was thrown into a pile of dead bodies that decomposed each day before Lily's eyes. Lily became disillusioned and unwilling to fight for survival. She became quite weak and sick and contracted typhus. Because she developed gangrene in her leg, she could not walk at the time of her liberation.

At liberation, Lily was transported to a nearby camp. Later, the Belgian Red Cross sent her home to Belgium, where she reunited with her aunt. Eventually she emigrated to join her father and his second family in the United States, where she met her future husband. They married three months later and have had three sons and six grandchildren.

America gave Lily the opportunity to be a human being again: "We were not lazy—we built a new family and a new life. And I am grateful for every day. But now it is up to us to tell the world what happened, to bear witness, and for the new generations and generations after us to see that we should never have another Hitler."

Lily currently lives with her husband half the year in Florida and half in Delaware.

HOW LILY M. COPED

Lily experienced not only psychological stress from fear and dehumanization but also the physical stress of hunger, typhoid and gangrene, not to mention the daily traumas of impending death. With no one to care for her and no one for her to love, if it hadn't been for the luck of liberation at her lowest ebb, she would not have survived. Even after the compound stresses she faced in the hospital and her later emigration to an unknown father and stepmother in America, she managed to cope and survive by forming a new affiliation with her husband-to-be. As many survivors learned in Auschwitz and carried through to later life, an affiliation or early marriage was a coping necessity.

Lily's affiliations with her aunt, with the Belgian girls with whom she traveled from Birkenau to Auschwitz and with Christiane demonstrate how she used emotion-focused coping strategies. "I had promised the other girl that I was going to take care of her, because we were separated from the other group, from the other Belgian people. So it felt like a duty, that she was part of me, and I kind of protected her. And . . . I guess that gave me the strength to carry on, because I kind of worried about her." The affiliation with others was mutual in that Lily protected other women and other women protected her in times of need.

Lily escaped Mengele's "death claws" because of the assistance of others. "And if it wouldn't have been for those two girls who were holding me, I would have collapsed. And I thought any moment he (Mengele) was going to shoot me or tell me to get on his jeep. I thought he was going to put . . . take me away." These relationships demonstrate mutual concern, protection and caring and served as a motive for survival and adaptation. The emotion-focused coping strategy of affiliation also characterizes Lily's valiant and compassionate act of stealing food to feed the starving Hungarian Jews in the camp. This action might have been an act of resistance, but surely it was a gift of hope and caring for others.

Lily also used emotion-focused coping strategies in her hopeful thoughts and her belief that she would eventually return to her remaining aunt in Belgium. By drawing upon techniques such as intellectualization and faith, Lily discovered a means of adaptation. She also coped by questioning the "meaning" of the atrocities she endured, and she experienced some relief in crying and struggling to "face the morning." Such means of coping suggest benefits from fantasizing that things might be better, but they also indicate that Lily strove to understand (meaning) how God could allow such pain and genocide in a world in which others lived in freedom.

PHONE INTERVIEW WITH LILY M.

Lily believed she coped by living one day at a time. There was no "future" and coping could only occur from hour to hour. "You never knew what the next hour would bring. . . . Never knew what the future was." Lily was certain she did not want to die and that each day she maintained her strength moved her one day closer to liberation.

"Friends . . . kept you strong," she believed, and she and other girls determined to help each other had formed a group in Mechelen. All of these girls had lost their mothers and had only each other to depend on for support and encouragement. "We were like sisters."

Lily spoke of the importance of being with her own thoughts. Dangerous as it was, she snuck out of the barrack at night and crept behind the buildings to the back corner where it was quiet. It was dark there, and safe from the lights of the watchtower, and she would stay there by herself, looking at the sky and talking to the stars. Lily tried to reason with G–d and thought about those who were free, wondering if they knew about the suffering and horrors of Auschwitz.

Lily spoke about her protection of Christiane and the promise she had made to "keep an eye" on the frail girl. "If you were by yourself, you would lose the battle." Taking care of someone else gave Lily the strength to persevere and to survive. The affiliation and support she gave to others, as well as the support of others for her, were vital to her resiliency.

Lily is a strong woman who was raised to care for others. She still wonders why the atrocities of the Holocaust happened, and she has never understood the meaning of the senseless suffering.

Through the Eyes of Lily M.

But inside of us, we will never be the same as any other person who has never been in a concentration camp. It isn't possible. Because of what we went through. Because there's not a day that (goes) by that we don't think of camp or of death. And of what we had to go through in life. . . . It was just terrible how we lived. It was so inhumane. Animals were taken care of better . . . had better love and care than we did. I remember . . . when I came into Auschwitz . . . such a hell place. . . . The ashes flew down from the crematorium on us. We were living with death all the time. And the smell, the odor. It was impossible to describe it. And I cannot believe . . . the people . . . outside of the camps, who lived around there . . . didn't know. I cannot believe that they . . . didn't know

*what went on. Because they must. If we smelled it, they
smelled it; and if the ashes fell on us, it must have fallen on
them, too, when the winds carried it away. . . . And each time
I hear a siren ring, to this day—even after forty-five years—I
still am right back in the war. And each time, when I go into
New York and when we drive . . . and I see the factories with
the chimneys, with the fires burning, I'm right back (with) the
ovens of the crematorium. It is always in my heart. It always
will be. Till I die. This is how we lived, from the death. And
the world was quiet. And never said a word.*

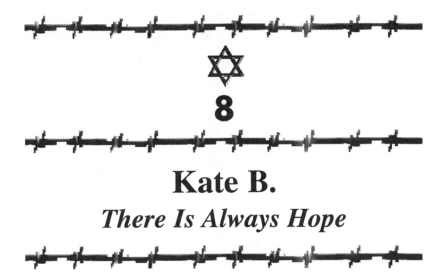

Kate B.
There Is Always Hope

ate B. was born to a middle-class Jewish family on August 27, 1927, in Szikszo, Hungary. She had a happy childhood as one of three children, and she always felt protected and shielded by her parents. Her family heard rumors about what was occurring during the occupation by the Nazis and, like many others, thought the rumors were exaggerations. The family believed the Nazis would never harm the Hungarian Jews because they were loyal citizens and because their fathers and grandfathers had fought for the country.

In March 1944 the Germans occupied Szikszo. They then ordered all Jews to wear the yellow Star of David and restricted their travel, business ventures, schooling and curfews. Within a few weeks all the Jews in Kate's town were rounded up and sent to the ghetto in Kassa (Kosice, Czechoslovakia). The Jewish families were not allowed to bring many personal possessions. Kate reported her family spent four weeks in the Kassa ghetto.

While living in the ghetto, the Jews attempted to make the best of a bad situation. Kate became "semi-officially engaged" to a young man, but soon the ghetto was liquidated. Three days later, on May 18, 1944, the family arrived in Auschwitz. Kate reported that the train ride was "so humiliating and . . . horrible. All they can do is cry or pray or try to soothe each other and, and sitting down on the floor and mothers with their children and . . . resting their heads in their laps . . . at least we were together." Upon entrance to Auschwitz, the men and women were separated. Kate remembered that a German officer asked her mother her age and she reported "Vierzig" (forty) and was "sent to the other side. But at that point we thought we were going to see each other later. I mean we had no idea of, of . . . what was waiting for us. And then they told us that you're going to see them later, that you're going to see them at night." Kate was taken to the showers, and her mother was placed in the line of death and exterminated in a gas chamber.

The Blockälteste in charge of the barrack where Kate was sent was Czechoslovakian. Kate remembered how she attempted to orient the young girls, telling them of the camp routine and that they would never see their parents again.

"You might as well forget about it because they are already in the . . . marched into the gas chambers. We just couldn't believe them, you know, in our wildest dream, that something like this could happen. We thought they were just . . . being rude to us. They . . . wanted to punish us for, for not being here the same way like they were for so many years already." Kate remembered they were told to volunteer if given the opportunity, that it would help them get out of Auschwitz, out of the death camp. Three days later guards moved Kate to the Plaszow camp in Krakow because there was not enough room for all the newcomers to Auschwitz.

Plaszow was even worse than Auschwitz, and Kate worked very hard physically. Appells were done in the freezing cold, and prisoners were forced to carry big wooden planks up a very steep mountain at a very quick pace. If the prisoners did not work quickly, they would miss the food, which was of limited supply. "From the other campmates who were, who were not . . . not good to us because they felt that we were . . . spoiled . . . or we were just coming from . . . our . . . homes. They were already suffering for years and years and they thought we're not even Jewish . . . prisoners because you don't speak the language (Yiddish). We don't belong."

On August 5, 1944, as Allied troops neared Plaszow, Kate was transferred back to Auschwitz. After three days in a transport, she was actually thankful to be back in Auschwitz. She was placed in

Lager C, shaved and tattooed. "We really didn't care at that point. We . . . ceased to be human beings. We were just a number already." Kate tried to avoid the selections, but she and her cousin finally volunteered for one. The Nazis needed five hundred women and selected Kate and one of her cousins. Two other cousins remained in Auschwitz, where, Kate later discovered, they perished.

Kate and her cousin were sent to work in a factory in Augsburg, Germany. They were told the factory belonged to Messerschmidt. German civilians worked there with the five hundred Hungarian girls who were locked up and lived in the factory building. Kate reported that this "work camp" was a little more humane than Auschwitz. However, when the nightly air raids occurred, the German guards, fearful the Jews might signal the airplanes, rushed the prisoners back to their barracks. On one occasion, a bomb fell in the courtyard and the Germans believed the end was in sight. The prisoners attempted to make some alterations to the chemicals and parts within the factory. They managed to sabotage the materials a little and "manipulate(d) a little that it shouldn't be so good, but I don't know."

Everyone tried to keep each other's spirits up during these times. Fantasizing was common, and discussions centered around what would occur when the girls were liberated. "I never thought for a minute that I'm really going to die. I . . . it just did not sink in. I mean with all these horrors around me . . . I always thought that we were dreaming of, of things—when I got home I'm going to do this and I'm going to do that and I just want to see this, this war end and just live for the day when we see the Germans defeated."

Suicide was always an option. "All you had to do is reach out for the electrified barbed-wire fence. But we will not do them the favor. We said if they want to kill us, they'll have to kill us. We are going to fight. We are going to stay alive. We had hope for the future."

Toward the end of the war, Kate was transferred to various camps. She ended up in Mühldorf, which was under the jurisdiction of the Dachau camp. Kate remembered the bombing and that she was happy the Germans were being bombed. The Swiss Red Cross eventually liberated the group on May 1, 1945, and took Kate and the others to Feldafing, which was originally a Hitler youth camp.

Kate returned to Hungary after the war, in September, and discovered that one brother had survived. Kate heard that her oldest brother had been killed on a death march in the last days of the war. She was reunited with her fiancé, also a survivor. They left Hungary because of the continued hostility and anti-Semitism there, and they married in Germany in 1946 in a displaced persons' camp. The couple emigrated to the United States in 1949.

"We are happy . . . of course we miss our families terribly and we never forget about them. It is part of our lives. . . . No matter how much we don't want to, whenever I get together with my friends or relatives, the subject comes up. We always wind up in the concentration camp." But, Kate added, "I am most proud to have outlived Hitler and the Nazis."

Kate and her husband had a son and a daughter and four grandchildren. She and her husband owned a restaurant for many years and retired together. Kate's husband authored eight books, including five on the Holocaust.

HOW KATE B. COPED

Kate believed her affiliations with her cousins and friends were vital in her coping during the Holocaust. She reported that hope was an essential element of her emotion-focused coping. She viewed herself as an optimist and believed that a person must never lose hope, even in the face of atrocities. "I always felt that no matter how much . . . front we're going to put up . . . at the end they're going to kill us. . . . But we did not give up hope. We didn't go around saying I'm going to lie down and die."

Kate coped by imagining and fantasizing that the war would soon be over. She relished her belief that the Germans would someday lose the war. She believed that one day she would be reunited with her friends, her parents and those she loved. Kate testified to the importance of her determination and inner perseverance: "It was so easy in Auschwitz. All you had to do is reach out for the barbed wires . . . we will not do them the favor. We said if they want to kill us, they'll have to kill us . . . because if we knew that our parents would be alive . . . we can do it . . . we are going to stay alive."

Kate noted that she had become numb during her internment. She also stated that luck and fate played roles in her survival.

PHONE INTERVIEW WITH KATE B.

Kate had no specific coping strategies, but everyone was in the same situation. She and her friends fantasized about the old days and hoped that they would eventually awaken from the horrors and return home to Hungary. Kate was aided by her cousins and friends, and she knew it was important to have such affiliations, which strengthened their survival. It was common for the girls to assist each other by keeping each other optimistic and not allowing one another to become depressed or negative. They would huddle together to share body warmth when temperatures dropped below freezing.

Kate suggested that she "went along with the flow. . . . I was young and pretty strong and did not ever give up." She believed that her childhood instilled her with self-confidence and that her religion and culture aided her belief that she was "good, no matter what they did to us." Kate's inner perseverance and belief that she was strong physically and emotionally were driving forces in her emotion-focused coping.

Kate mentioned she did not always foresee what would occur and became emotionally numbed during the massive traumatization. In light of all that she mentioned, Kate was very emphatic when stating that luck and fate played a large part in her survival during the Holocaust.

Through the Eyes of Kate B.

People should be vigilant all the time not to, not to think that, this really doesn't matter. All these . . . hate mongers . . . if you let it get out of hand, then this can happen (again). Never lose hope. Where there is life, there is always hope.

Cecilie K.
A Poet's Heart

ecilie K. was born on April 13, 1925, in Yasinya (Jasina), Czechoslovakia, and was the youngest of four sisters and two brothers. Her father was a foreign-language and math teacher within their small community. Her parents also owned a grocery store that her mother ran. Her orthodox family was very close to one another. When she was nine, Cecilie's father passed away.

The Hungarians occupied Yasinya when she was fourteen. First, the Jews were not allowed to go to school. Then, one day when she returned from a friend's house, she discovered that one of her sisters, Feige, had been imprisoned and sent to Budapest.

The family concocted a plan for Cecilie, who could pass as non-Jewish, to travel on a train to Budapest. They accomplished this by purchasing a first-class ticket, which was not allowed as seating for Jews, and by buying a known anti-Semitic newspaper for Cecilie to read on the train. The goal of the trip was for Cecilie to gain legal assistance for her sister from a lawyer in Budapest. Upon arrival in Budapest, she learned that Feige had been transported to Backa Topola in Serbia. Cecilie worked to earn money, arranged a means of travel and went to find her sister.

Cecilie, still only fourteen and now alone, hired a lawyer, arranged for Feige's release, and went to live six miles away with her mother and married sister Mina. After she was released, Feige learned that her mother and Cecilie had already gone to Mina's. Cecilie later learned that Feige was arrested again and perished in one of the camps.

After living in hiding for a year, Cecilie, Mina, and their mother were deported and placed in cattle cars heading to Auschwitz. No one attempted to escape because there "was absolutely no way or no chance" to get away. They believed not that they were being transported for annihilation but that they would survive.

They thought nothing could be worse than what they had experienced in the ghetto, but upon arrival in Auschwitz they were told quickly by whispering Kapos that women with children, the elderly and the unfit would be exterminated. "Listen, if you have children then give them away to older people because women with children, anybody older, is going to be killed. They are killing the same night. There is no chance for these people to survive."

In a quick "choiceless choice" to help her daughter survive, Cecilie's mother took Mina's son, her grandson, in her arms. Guards then pushed her into the line assigned for death. As Cecilie's mother joined this "line of death," she yelled to Cecilie, "Not to worry and take care of your sister." Thereafter, Cecilie felt an obligation "and a double challenge to keep my sister Mina alive."

While retelling the horrors and dehumanizing conditions she experienced upon arrival at Auschwitz, Cecilie spoke of the demoralizing conditions and of the Kapos telling them that their mothers, sisters and fathers were being burned in the smoke filling the skies above their heads. She protected her sister from this horrible fact by telling her that the guards were doing this only to scare those who were vulnerable. "They shoved us into the showers . . . first they opened the hot water so we got scalded and then they opened the cold water . . . we were running out and we were beaten with the whips."

"The things that we have witnessed is—is unbelievable what human beings can do to other human beings. Even animals have a tendency to kill only—they would kill only for food, but they (Nazis) killed for pleasure." Continually becoming weaker and weaker, Cecilie's goal was to keep her sister alive and to bear witness to the atrocities that occurred during internment. Despite her sister's constant desire to commit suicide, Cecilie perceived that it was her daily responsibility to convince her sister to live for another day. "She would say she doesn't want to live. She wants to go to the wires . . . so each time I would tell her, not today. We always have time to kill ourselves. . . . But I wanted very much to live."

A Blockälteste favored Cecilie and took her and her sister into the children's block. She often asked Cecilie to recite poems for her. Cecilie decided to curry the favor of the Blockälteste by writing a poem about what a wonderful and beautiful person she was. The Blockälteste liked it so much that she brought her SS boyfriend to hear this tribute. In her testimony, Cecilie confided that the poem was the only poem she ever wrote, that it was a lie. She pushed it from her mind so that today she cannot even remember it. Yet because of that poem, the Blockälteste continued to protect Cecilie and Mina during selections by hiding them under blankets in an empty room in the block. One day the guards cleared out the entire block and marched everyone to the gas chamber. Cecilie remembered hearing a guard say that the gas chambers were full and that members of the SS decided to "switch their group" with a group being deported to an ammunition work camp in Nuremberg. Cecilie remembered the SS guards deciding to "make a switch. We'll take these to work, and the other group we will take to the gas chamber." Cecilie believed she continued to live on that day due purely to luck.

The SS moved Cecilie and Mina to a subcamp of Flossenburg (Siemens-Schukert Werke), where they worked in an ammunition factory. When the Allies began bombing that area, the prisoners were sent to Holleischen (a subcamp of Ravensbruck), another ammunition factory, until liberation by a few Russian partisans, and later the British.

After liberation, Mina emigrated to Israel. Cecilie reunited with Joe (her fiancé prior to deportation to Auschwitz) on a train trip to Budapest, and they married on August 21, 1945. While living in Czechoslovakia, Cecilie was hospitalized with pleurisy. "I prayed for death. I had no desire to live. I could not imagine how I can possibly go on living without my family. I loved them so much, we were so close. I couldn't understand why I fought so much to live in virtual hell, where I was starved and beaten and faced death daily. . . . I had love, food and a home, and I lost interest. I was only twenty years old." With Joe's support, nurturing and encouragement, Cecilie recovered and lived with Joe, her brother-in law and Mina. Joe worked as a dental technician with his brother-in law.

In 1948, after the birth of their son Peter, Cecilie and Joe emigrated to the United States. "I gave birth to a little boy, and he became the focus of our life, our miracle." After living in the United States for a short time, Cecilie received a diagnosis of tuberculosis, her son was placed in a foster home for fear of infection and Cecilie was placed in a sanatorium.

Cecilie left the hospital eighteen months later and moved into an apartment with her husband and son. Mina came to America to help with Peter. Because of Cecilie's weakened condition, and a relapse in her condition, Peter returned with Mina to Israel for six months while Cecilie continued her recovery. "After another year and a half of treatment in the sanatorium, I was reunited with my son, and I had to learn to cope and accept what could not be changed. . . . I made an effort to reshape my life."

Cecilie participated in various community activities and religious groups. She attended college classes and "even learned how to smile; however, the pain, the sadness, the emptiness never left me."

While viewing a television documentary in Israel, Mina saw evidence that confirmed the girls' mother had died in the crematorium. She also learned of a recently discovered diary of a German soldier who had photographed prisoners' arrivals and exterminations in Auschwitz. Mina watched as images of her and Cecilie flashed on the television screen. Though shocked by that vision, she was also confronted with a group photo of her family's transport into Auschwitz. As the documentary continued, she saw a photo of a woman holding a young boy just before they were exterminated in the gas chamber. Mina, traumatized again by this time, realized this was a photograph of her son in the arms of her mother moments before entering the gas chambers. Today, the United States Holocaust Memorial Museum exhibits that picture, enlarged to human size, where visitors proceed out of an authentic cattle car that transported prisoners to the gates of Auschwitz.

Cecilie and Joe had three children and eight grandchildren. Cecilie has been very active with the United States Holocaust Memorial Museum and is a frequent speaker. She also has spoken at the World Conference of Survivors in Israel and has written two books on the Holocaust. All of the proceeds from her books are donated to the United States Holocaust Memorial Museum in Washington, D.C.

In 1985 Joe died of cancer. Cecilie remarried another survivor in 1988, and recently he died from cancer. Her older sister Perl lives on the East Coast. Cecilie continues to stay active socially and physically, visiting her sister Mina in Israel every year.

Cecilie noted, "We, the survivors, are diminishing with each passing day. Before the curtain falls, I am reflecting upon our lives, the failures, successes and accomplishments. We endured tortures and brutalities, but our determination to live and cheat the gas chambers became the focus of our daily struggle. Miraculously we returned from the cinders of Auschwitz with the expectation that the world would hold the murderers accountable for their crimes. To our dismay the survivors were received with marked silence and hostility while the murderers were given sanctuary! The survivors, emotionally devastated, bereft of family and stripped of all worldly possessions, found solace only in each other. Our friends were survivors, and we married survivors. Who else could have understood our searing pain, our nightmares, our irreplaceable loss and emptiness? We forged ahead to build new families and a better life. We worked hard and made great strides in every facet of life, including literature, science, art, politics and economics. Our greatest achievements, however, are our precious children and grandchildren. We gave them our unconditional love and instilled in them the fine qualities and pride of their ancestors. Our children filled the void in our hearts and they helped mend our shattered lives. In their hands we place the torch of remembrance. To mankind we leave our recorded histories and memorials to serve as a reminder of how hate, bigotry and persecution can destroy millions of innocent adults and children. We hope that our tragedies will teach a lesson in tolerance, compassion and respect for every race, creed and religion, thus creating a better world to live in for future generations."

HOW CECILIE K. COPED

Cecilie's testimony illustrates her frequent use of problem-focused coping strategies. Her oral history reveals a variety of situations in which she believed she could affect the environment and create change. These included such actions as riding a train to save her sister, stealing bread and potatoes for survival, withstanding beatings to assist her depressed sister, and hiding from the selections in Auschwitz.

Keeping her sister alive and continuing her relationship with her sister were primary in Cecilie's testimony. Determined to keep each other alive, Cecilie and her sister demonstrated the adaptation strategy of affiliation as a means of survival.

On a few occasions, Cecilie spoke about luck and hope, which illustrated her utilization of emotion-focused coping. She reported that she was designated to "be the hope" of the women sent to the subcamp and that luck saved her from the gas chamber in Auschwitz.

PHONE INTERVIEW WITH CECILIE K.

Cecilie believed she remained alive because of her dedication to keeping her sister alive. "My attention was on her." Her sister wanted to commit suicide, and Cecilie felt responsible for preventing that. She also felt the Blockälteste's protection was vital to her survival. She believed she avoided a selection in which she would surely have been exterminated because of the Blockälteste's protection.

Cecilie reported that one "had to stop thinking about the past and your family. You could only survive if you think 'I want to live.'" She said she thought of nothing except protecting her sister, her friends and herself. "You had to have someone to hold on to!"

Cecilie remembered one young girl who was a talented dancer. Forced to dance "in this hell," she was taken away for three days and was unrecognizable upon her return. The young girl had been beaten, raped and tortured. Cecilie reported how she protected her young friend by placing her between herself and her sister during a selection. The dancer was chosen to die in that selection, and Cecilie wrote a poem in memory of her.

The poems that Cecilie wrote were an emotional outlet, and they also were a means of connecting with the Blockälteste, who encouraged her talent and protected her as much as possible. On occasion, the Blockälteste asked her to read her poems in front of an SS guard. This favored status aided her in her survival.

"Auschwitz was a different world." The dehumanizing conditions, the beatings, the mistreatment led to a hardening of survivors. After liberation, it was difficult for Cecilie to feel and "become human" again.

Through the Eyes of Cecilie K.

We hope that future generations will never have the experience . . . (that) what we went through, will absolve all generations to come in the future. And all we hope is only that we are leaving behind, we the survivors, are leaving behind some meager tools—books, tapes and Holocaust museums. We want the future generations to know, to go to the museums; and when they look at those little shoes, that they will know that to us these are precious because they belonged once to our children. They belonged to my family. We lost so much. Nothing can (ever) make this right. . . . We survived; but our lives were destroyed. Because though we look like you, we can never be like you.

We wear nice clothes like you. We go on vacations like you. We make beautiful affairs. But affairs that I made, a lot of friends arrived, but the ones I wanted most, they never arrived. And we go to funerals and we cry for the ones that we never buried. . . . Remember the survivors. We are the last ones. Remember everyone because when we are gone, people will say it never happened.

Many years ago, I witnessed the massacre of my people and when my turn came, I wasn't thrown into the flames like all the others. Instead, I was chopped up into small pieces, but I refused to die. I picked up all the pieces, put them neatly together, made myself look like a real person, but in fact, remained a mummy.

I returned to the world in great anticipation, to witness the severe punishment the world would heap on the murderers. To my surprise, the world judged the victims. Watching with my mummy eyes, I saw the unbelievable. People protesting that they did not want to see those horrible pictures, that this could not have happened in the twentieth century, in civilized Europe. Then came the witnesses, telling their experiences, and echoes came to my mummy ears—exaggeration: propaganda! So the victims were condemned for disturbing the peace and the case was closed. We the mummies knew the truth, that no pictures can portray the reality, that no book holds enough pages to describe and record the suffering and the ruthless murder of loved ones. We, the surviving mummies, took the matter into our hands. We looked at the pictures ourselves, read the books in silence and decided to keep mum, too. We had to fit into the world. Even when my children would ask me, 'Mommy, why are you crying?' I would answer, 'Just a headache, my dears.' So, who am I? Cecilie K., living amongst you with a slight headache.

From *Sentenced to Live* by Cecilie Klein, New York: Holocaust Library, 1988.

Guta W.

Narrow Escapes and Constant Courage

uta W. (who requested that her full name, Guta Blass Weintraub, be used in this book) was born on January 22, 1924, in Lodz, Poland. She remembered having a happy childhood in a loving family. Her father owned a factory in which he was a pattern maker for military-school and boy-scout uniforms. Her upper middle-class family was able to send her and her younger brother to Jewish private schools.

Anti-Semitism was prominent in Poland, but Guta heard only occasionally about someone being beaten up or of a synagogue being burned or vandalized. Guta was sheltered from news of unpleasant incidents by her parents.

In September 1939 the Germans invaded Lodz. They began occupying and taking over school buildings, business offices, and government offices and settled themselves in Guta's private high school. The school closed because of fear for the safety of the girls after it became clear that the Polish army was running eastward to avoid being encircled by the approaching German army. The Polish army actually retreated through Lodz when unsuccessful in attempts to contain the Germans' advances.

Guta's family remained in Lodz until December 1939, when Guta's father decided it was too dangerous to stay. To evade the Germans, the family went to Guta's mother's hometown of Wierzbnik-Starachowice. To survive, even in hiding, the family pretended they were not Jewish. Guta's father spoke perfect German, as did Guta, who spoke with an authentic German accent. The ability to speak in the native tongue assisted the family to appear as if they were of German or mixed-German descent.

Later, the family rented an apartment, and Guta's father continued his work as a clothing designer, making military clothes and sportswear. Guta, now sixteen, opened her own kindergarten and cared for Jewish children of parents who were still capable of working.

Upon establishment of the ghetto of Wierzbnik, Guta's family was able to move about freely inside the areas of confinement. It was most important to them that they were able to be together. "Our lives were still sort of normal because we were able to get together with friends, with relatives, and an amazing thing all through our confinements in the ghetto or in a work camp or even in a concentration camp is the fact that . . . the Jewish population always had a sense of wanting to learn . . . wanting to have knowledge, so we did not stop." Guta continued to teach kindergarten inside the ghetto and others were able to teach Guta. She remembered that she took classes in Latin and French during this period. "We were not torn apart, and therefore . . . life seemed to be normal. It was very special . . . because we valued each other . . . we just understood it better because family ties were very close among Jewish families. . . . We did not have the million *things* that we had before, but it did not seem to matter."

With the situation worsening inside Poland, the family prepared for evacuation and Guta's father packed knapsacks for each of them with essential clothes and money, in case anyone was separated from the others. This preparation was helpful when the Germans came at 4:00 A.M. one morning and gathered the Jews in the marketplace. Forced into a selection, the younger and stronger people remained and were distributed into three work camps in the city.

Though initially separated from her father and mother, Guta reunited with them when a Jewish policeman, watching the selection, realized what was happening and took Guta's parents to her from another line. The Jewish policeman told Guta's brother that he and the policeman's son should volunteer to be stationed outside the city so they could work as cleaning boys and helpers to Polish citizens. Guta, her father and her mother were taken to a woodwork-factory work camp. Guta met her future husband—who was very handsome, clever and gathered food for the family—at this camp. "He was . . . always able to . . . manage things. He was very . . . how to say? . . . innovative?"

During Guta's time in the working camp, a Ukrainian soldier took a liking to her. This soldier, named Schrot, got drunk and came running through the barrack one night, calling for Guta and shouting that if she did not appear, he would kill everyone within the barrack. Guta talked cleverly to the drunken soldier, and eventually he left with everyone unharmed.

Soon after, the SS took Guta and her family to Majowka, a work camp that housed a steel factory. They were the last ones to arrive in the camp, and they were met by the same guard, Schrot. Schrot demanded that the group divide while forced to walk to a mass grave. "Women on one side, men on the other side. Make a line in fours." Guta remembered, "Then he stood at the end of the grave and said to us, 'You have one minute.' He said it in German. He said, 'You have one minute to say your prayers. You'll be shot.' . . . But my utmost feeling and reaction was my concern, first of all, for my parents, for my brother, for my friends, for everybody there." Guta ran out toward the soldier and jumped on his back and put her fingers around his throat and began choking him. The two fell to the ground, where German soldiers pulled them apart. A young girl (who later became her sister-in-law) cried out that someone needed to assist Guta, who had fainted. The soldier took a gun and shot Guta: "It was from an angle coming here and going out this way. So it basically grazed my skin and part of my bone since my head was that way." Guta played dead while bleeding profusely, and a Ukrainian soldier checked to see if she had died. "And I was still in the same position . . . he wanted to see if I have (a) pulse. To this day a doctor has difficulty finding (my) pulse, so he didn't find it. . . . He picked up my arm, I felt a release, so I dropped it like it was a piece of wood."

Left for dead in the midst of a Russian bombing, Guta escaped while still bleeding profusely and crawled to the nearby barrack where her family had been transferred during the chaotic situation near the grave site. "Well, the only thing that I can do is just get under the barrack. Little by little, I got myself under the barrack and they were even lower than my body could . . . take it, so I had to . . . squeeze myself in. I felt, every time I breathed, I felt that I'm raising the floor of the barrack."

Upon hearing her parents' voices the next morning, Guta came out of hiding and joined them. They all burst into tears of joy. Her parents thought she had been killed. Her wounds were tended to, and for a few days they were happy and together.

Upon learning that Guta was alive, Schrot came running into the barrack, waving his gun again. He screamed, "If she doesn't come out I will start with her relatives and I'll shoot you all." Guta believed her life had little meaning at that point and she came forward. Schrot grabbed her hand and pulled her out of the barrack, behind the barbed wire, and into a wood storeroom. He locked her in the warehouse, where she was discovered by a German officer who beat her with a rifle and then sent her to the hospital to be bandaged and sent back to her family.

Shortly after, in September 1944, Guta and her family traveled on wagons to Auschwitz. Guta and her mother were separated quickly into lines of males and females and sent to the showers. At the request of a friend, Guta hid gold pieces in a bar of soap.

The women exited the showers, all of them naked, then endured a selection by Adolph Eichmann, some Ukrainians and two German women. Guta felt humiliated and totally devastated. She rushed to Eichmann, who was in charge, and begged to be placed with her mother, from whom she had been separated. She pleaded that her mother was the only person left in her life. She promised to be loyal and work harder next to her mother, and Eichmann placed them together. The line, however, was going directly to the gas chamber.

"Well, the girl (German girl in the selection group) somehow took pity on me. . . . With this girl I had several other incidents, too, because I must say that as bad as they were, I wouldn't want to say anything special for the Germans as a whole, but . . . I must say that on occasions, you found a person with feelings and compassion and they did special things." Guta pleaded with the German girl, "If this was happening to you, wouldn't you want to save your mother?" The German girl was touched by Guta and smuggled her and her mother to the line that was sent to the barracks. The next morning, Guta was tattooed with the number A-14028 and her mother with A-14029.

The gas chambers could not be worked fast enough to liquidate all of the Jews, so Guta and her family remained in the cramped, temporary barrack with nine or ten other women. There was no work that had any purpose. "Even though there was work, it had no meaning. It just had meaning to destroy us, to make us tired, to make us exhausted, because in the beginning like, for example, every morning we had to be woken up at four o'clock." Each day began with the morning Appell and the counting of prisoners.

Guta and her mother worked with a group that moved stones from one location to another. Moving the rocks had no purpose except to exhaust and humiliate the prisoners. This process of physically torturing and exhausting the prisoners saved bullets and worked as efficiently.

Guta remained in Auschwitz from September 1944 through January 1945, when she and the other prisoners were sent on a death march. At the time of the departure, rumors spread quickly about assassination attempts on Hitler and about the German guards poisoning all of the bread in the camp. "We heard of many other things and that's when they, instead of running themselves, they had to take us because they did not want to leave any evidence, especially evidence that can talk."

Guta remembered being chased out of the camp for the death march and that everything happened very quickly. Transportation, which was privately owned, was not available, and Guta and other prisoners were forced to walk in groups of thirty or forty on a road covered with bodies of men who had died on the road before Guta's group departed from Auschwitz. "And we saw a leg or a hand or a nose sticking out from the . . . from the snow, and we realized that this is what happened. So it made our journey that much worse because we wanted to see when we saw somebody if it was . . . my father, my brother, or somebody else, whatever."

On January 22, 1945, Guta's twenty-first birthday, the group boarded open-platform cars headed to Ravensbruck. Guta reported that her mother's physical health was worsening.

Her mother quickly became too weak to leave the Ravensbruck barrack by herself, so Guta and a girlfriend held her up during roll call. Once again Guta was aided by the young German girl, who instructed Guta to take her mother into the barrack. "I picked up my mother in my arms like a baby, and I walked with her into the barrack, and I sat in the chair and I was just holding her, like a baby." Guta's mother had a stroke that day and was taken to the hospital.

That afternoon, Guta brought her own portion of food to her hospitalized mother and was informed that she was dead. "I was just like a . . . like a puppet doing things, and the first things were I took all her belongings, her shoes, her little scarf, her garter belt, her comb and whatever else she had there, and . . . still I knew that this was not enough of her that I wanted to take with me. And I asked for scissors and I cut a great part of her hair— and I did it, amazingly, only from the left side because I said, 'It is from the heart side'—and I cut her hair, and I still have it."

Guta began mourning her dead mother and returned to her body the next day to once again say a final farewell. To maintain her silence during this final visit to her mother's corpse, Guta stuffed her fist in her mouth so that, in her misery, she would not scream out loud.

Later, the SS forced Guta to work in an area where human waste was turned into fertilizer for German farmers. Guta and others were forced to stand in narrow ditches while stirring the waste with large sticks or shovels. "(The) smell was horrible . . . people sometimes fell up to their necks and nobody bothered taking them out. So it was . . . unforgettable. It was a horrible, horrible . . . if you had to imagine a horror story, you couldn't."

By this time, Guta was depleted emotionally. Still, she volunteered to be placed on a list supposedly intended for the Swedish Red Cross. Having been deceived by the Germans in other situations, she knew that volunteering oftentimes meant certain death. "But I didn't care. I did not care to live anymore. I couldn't live with the memories and I certainly could not see the future, so I put myself on the list." The list actually was given to a Swedish

Red Cross liberation group, and Guta was transported by them to Denmark, and thereafter to Sweden.

After the war, Guta emigrated to the United States and currently lives on the East Coast.

HOW GUTA W. COPED

Guta's devotion to her family, especially her mother, is a prime example of emotion-focused coping centered around relationships with others, and, clearly, it was Guta's primary motivation. Guta risked her life on numerous occasions to save her loved ones. "My concern (was) first of all for my parents, for my brother, for my friends, for everybody there." She protected her group from Schrot by calming the drunken SS soldier after he threatened to kill the entire barrack of Jews if Guta did not do as he asked. By placing herself at risk, daring even to jump upon an SS guard's back, she saved her mother and other prisoners on the brink of death at a mass grave.

Guta reported no problem-focused coping and suggested that she obtained assistance from girlfriends and other prisoners, as well as from the young German girl who saved her from death a few times.

PHONE INTERVIEW WITH GUTA W.

Guta emphasized that Auschwitz's purpose was to dehumanize the Jewish people. "The mentality of the camp cannot be understood . . . under any circumstances. The Holocaust was not simple at all . . . the mentality you cannot tell, unless you tell everything." She spoke of the Nazi mentality being like a fungus spread by Hitler and Nazi ideology.

Guta was determined and very lucky to survive. She and other Polish Jewish women were very strong physically and had strong and optimistic characters. Guta was devoted to her family, which she considered to be the norm in Eastern European Jewish families, and she was willing to do anything to protect her family from harm. Guta minimized her heroic deed at the edge of the mass grave. "I do not doubt that these people survived because of me. I did it like an impulse . . . because of my mother . . . it was just natural." Guta believed she survived because she did things to protect her mother that she would not normally do.

Guta coped with the extreme massive traumatization and protected her loved ones by pleading at the selection line with Eichmann, with the guard Schrot and with the young German girl. Dignity and respect for family were the primary motivating forces for her survival and adaptation.

Guta became numbed and depleted emotionally when her mother died in Ravensbruck only three weeks before liberation by the Swedish Red Cross. "I lost my will to live when my mother died."

11

Margaret K.
Despite the Odds

argaret K. was born on June 8, 1923, in Rogazin, a province in Posen, Germany. Her family adopted Germany as their homeland. Margaret was the youngest of ten children and remembered her childhood as very happy. She reported that her family was not very religious, that her father was a butcher and that her mother did not work. When Hitler came to power, the Gestapo took her brother Max, and the family could not discover what happened to him. Six months later the family was informed that Max had died in Sachsenhausen from a reported "infection."

Margaret was at her sister's house when the Germans came and took her to the police station. They interrogated her about others who might be hidden, and Margaret told them that she knew where other Jews were, "But I don't think that I will tell you, because you got me and this is enough." Angered by her resistance, the police placed her in a jail in Berlin, where she stayed for months. They decided that she would be transported to Auschwitz. Margaret reported, "My mind was made up. I didn't want to go. . . . I opened the window and I jumped out. I jumped out—it's the second floor. I didn't want to die. I just thought I could run away." Margaret broke her arm and leg in the attempted escape. One of the SS men who captured her outside the building wanted to send her on the transport to Auschwitz, and the other (who Margaret referred to as a "nice Nazi") decided she would be placed in a hospital instead. "So I got . . . I got lucky. So they brought me to—this was in Berlin, it was a Jewish hospital," which was in a Jewish camp where she stayed for nine months.

At the end of that time, in 1942, Margaret and thirty-nine other Jews from the camp were transported to Auschwitz. Upon arrival, Margaret and two other girls were chosen from the group.

They survived the transport. Margaret believed she was "plain lucky" escaping the selection. She was taken to the showers, shaved and placed in the barracks with many others from Holland. The group was forced into crowded conditions and to drink from one bowl, and many died very quickly from malnutrition.

Margaret was caught laughing during a roll call and was beaten by Irma Grese. She lost three teeth in the exchange. She remembered Mengele watching the prisoners march out and how the Jews were forced to "sing happy songs when we are marched through . . . this door" to work in the potato fields.

Margaret remained in Auschwitz for more than two years. She watched the crematorium ovens working twenty-four hours each day and the skies red from the flames that doomed others to death. Determined to make it through the atrocities of Auschwitz, Margaret told herself, "I have to get out of here. From there, I will never get out (ovens) because nobody came out of there alive."

After more than two years in the camp, Margaret was emotionally depleted and decided she would stop an SS man on the streets of the camp complex to request she be sent to work in Germany. Her friends begged her not to proceed with this plan. Margaret responded, "Well, what is the difference? I'm here so long. If I . . . get killed today, it's okay. I'm dead anyway." She told the SS guard she was German and had worked in an ammunition camp before she was transported, had heard that German girls were being sent to Berlin to work, and that she would like to take two friends with her. The guard told her to come to the SS barrack with the two other women.

After giving blood to the doctors in charge, the three were told they were doing a good deed. "I say, 'Why?' He said, 'This is for

German soldiers.' I say 'German . . . soldiers? I am Jewish.' So he says that the Jews are no good and that Jewish blood is no good." Then the guards took the women, in the dark, to another block. The three felt unsure whether they were being taken to the crematoria or not. Actually, they were taken to Czechoslovakia to work in an ammunition factory, where they were liberated after one year in May 1945.

Margaret was the only one within her family sent to the concentration camp who survived. When she returned to her home in Berlin, she learned she had lost twenty-four family members but that two of her three brothers had survived, one having gone to Shanghai and the other to Scotland.

In Berlin she soon met a survivor, Sal, whom she eventually married. Their daughter was born in Berlin in 1948. In 1949 the family emigrated to Israel but were not happy there, so they moved to the United States in 1955.

Margaret and her husband worked in factories while they lived in Georgia. They moved later to New Jersey to be with relatives, but after a short time they returned to Georgia, where they purchased a grocery store. Years later the couple purchased a delicatessen, which they owned for over eighteen years.

Margaret and Sal had two daughters and six grandchildren. The couple recently celebrated their fiftieth wedding anniversary. Margaret helps care for her grandchildren. Her husband continues to help at the delicatessen a few days a week.

HOW MARGARET K. COPED

Margaret estimated that her internment lasted four years, beginning with capture at her sister's house and placement in jail and continuing through her attempted escape, hospitalization, internment in Auschwitz and transport to a work camp in Czechoslovakia. During her years in Auschwitz, Margaret utilized both emotion-focused and problem-focused coping strategies. With problem-focused strategies, she manipulated her environment and created opportunities for change, as when she asked the SS guard to transfer her. She wanted to find a way "out" of Auschwitz and was not willing to sit and wait to leave through the chimneys of the oven crematorium. Margaret's emotion-focused coping shows in her relationships with other women and her protection of them. These relationships motivated and supported her will to survive within the camp.

Margaret noted that luck played a large part in her survival, as in her being chosen from the group of thirty-nine others to be saved. She also considered it luck that the SS guard allowed her to go into the Jewish hospital instead of placing her on a transport to Auschwitz.

PHONE INTERVIEW WITH MARGARET K.

Margaret persevered because of her will to survive the atrocities of the Nazi occupation and internment. "I didn't want to die. I'm a very, very tough cookie." She believed that being a "hard worker" in the potato fields helped her cope, as did the support of friends in her barrack. Her friendships with women were very important to Margaret, which is why she dared to speak to the SS guard about passage out of Auschwitz for herself and her friends. She remembered saying, "Well, I'm here long enough. If I'm going to die in their hands (the Nazis), then let me . . . then this is what I want."

Margaret demonstrated emotion-focused coping when she became so numb that she "didn't care anymore" and so determined that she was willing to risk asking the SS guard to help her leave the work camp.

12

Barbara F.
A Powerful Will

arbara F. was born on May 4, 1920, in Beliu, Romania, in North Transylvania. She was the youngest and only surviving child of her aging parents and, admittedly, was very spoiled and sheltered by her doting parents. Barbara reported thirty to thirty-five Jewish families in her very small Jewish community. The community rabbi taught the children Hebrew language, prayers and blessings on Sunday mornings.

Until 1937, Barbara's parents owned and operated a grocery store in Beliu. At that time, the community was friendly to Jews, with little anti-Semitic treatment within the community at large. That year the family sold their home and moved to Oradea, approximately seventy-five miles from Beliu. Here, the family also owned and operated a grocery store.

Barbara excelled in school and received many awards (medals) for her academic achievements. In 1940 she graduated from a Romanian school but was refused entry into the university due to anti-Jewish laws implemented by the Hungarian government, which by then controlled the area in which she lived. Barbara reported that her family had heard about the rising anti-Semitism in nearby European countries. They were "a little bit . . . scared, but everything happened far away from us. . . . We had radios, and we heard what is happening but we said, 'This can't happen to us.' We . . . were very optimistic . . . very foolishly optimistic."

In September 1940 Barbara went to work in the Jewish hospital in Oradea, where she trained as a laboratory assistant. She worked in this hospital until March 1944, when the Nazis occupied the country. The next month, Jews were ordered to wear a mandatory Star of David on their clothing. May 4, 1944, marked the beginning of ghettoization, and a ghetto was established in Oradea around the orthodox synagogue. A hospital was set up within the ghetto, and Barbara worked there with very little equipment.

On May 26, 1944, the Nazis began liquidating the ghetto, and many within the community were taken and transported to their death in Auschwitz. Barbara and her parents were deported in June 1944 and taken in cattle cars to Auschwitz, although they were told that they were going to work in the "puszta" (the Hungarian prairie).

Men and women were separated upon arrival, and Barbara remembered that Polish prisoners warned the arrivals, "Give the children to the old people, old womans." When Barbara's father was sent into a different line, Barbara and her mother were unable to say good-bye to him. Then Mengele directed that Barbara be separated from her mother, and she was placed forcibly in a different line. "I didn't have time to kiss my mother, or to see . . . to say something to her. I was in terrible shock. And after that we find out that the people, they . . . I mean, the women, they . . . all the people—I mean, mother and all the others—they then go direct to the gas chamber. And they . . . when we were around one . . . hundred or maybe more on the right side, they take us to the bath." After being processed and shaved, Barbara was moved to Lager C in Block 15. She was in shock, as was everyone else, crying and screaming as they realized the terrible reality of their situation.

The prisoners slept on straw on the floor. Mornings brought Appells and counting, which was done repeatedly due to errors—and as a means of additional torture.

Although numb from shock and horror, Barbara forced herself to eat to survive. In July she volunteered to carry containers to Lager B because she had been told she would receive some extra food at the completion of the task. During that work, some food spilled, and Barbara and two other girls were tortured for hours because of the spillage.

Later, Barbara was sent to Lager B during a selection of three hundred women who had experience doing fine handwork, such as tailors and lab technicians. She was quarantined for three weeks, then taken to Weisswasser, a subcamp of Gross-Rosen. She was interned in this work camp from October 1944 to February 1945. Though assigned at first to work in the chemistry lab, she was later transferred to the cathode workshop. The Nazis evacuated the camp as Russian troops approached, and Barbara and others were transported through many camps while the Nazis tried to avoid the Allied troops. The prisoners were liberated in 1945 near the German-Danish border at Padborg, where the Red Cross gave them food.

Upon liberation, Barbara weighed only sixty pounds. She was transported to Malmo, Sweden, and later she returned to her only surviving uncle in Romania. She studied at the university there from 1946 to 1951, during which time she met her husband-to-be. They married in 1950.

Upon graduation, Barbara became an industrial pharmacist and emigrated to Israel. While there, she worked at a hospital. Her husband worked as an accountant. The couple emigrated to the United States in 1968 and moved to Massachusetts.

HOW BARBARA F. COPED

Barbara reported very little in her testimony that relates to problem-focused or emotion-focused coping. However, she did volunteer to transport containers of food to increase her chances for survival, which illustrates a strong will to survive and problem-focused coping.

Barbara was numb from the trauma of losing her parents but mindful of what was happening. She noted that the meager food had a smell and realized it contained bromide to prevent the women from menstruating. Luck and her will to survive carried her through. Later, relationships in the work camp helped. When she became ill, a Jewish nurse, whom she stayed in touch with after the war, gave her extra food to strengthen her.

13

Toby S.
Protected by Her Peers

oby S. was born on July 15, 1920, in Mittelwischo, Transylvania, Romania. She was the youngest of six children and the only girl. Toby's childhood was a struggle, with her father dying five months before her birth. Her mother was only twenty-eight at the time, and her grandmother and relatives in America helped the family survive financially.

Toby attended a public school and then worked as a dressmaker. In 1939 she married a businessman and was "the happiest woman in the world." After three months of marriage, the Hungarians began to torture the Jews in the community. They did not allow Jews on the streets or on trains. When found on a train, a Jew would be punished by the loss of his or her tongue, hands, eyes or life. During this time, Jewish businesses were confiscated by the Communists and then run by Gentiles or the government.

One of Toby's uncles, a rabbi, was ordered to decide which of his two children he loved the best. Because he was unable to choose, the authorities killed one of his children, then the other, right in front of him, and finally the authorities killed the rabbi. Such atrocities continued, and Jews trying to save themselves and their families hid in the woods or elsewhere with the assistance of others. Gentiles hid Toby and her husband in a cellar. Soldiers eventually discovered their whereabouts and captured them. After bribing the soldiers with money, the couple was allowed to escape.

Toby's husband was later captured and interned in a concentration camp for six months. Toby was pregnant with their first child and thought she was a widow, so she moved in with her in-laws. In 1940 Hungary took over Romania, and Toby's husband returned home safely. Their child was born in March 1940, and the family lived safely until 1942. In 1942 Toby became pregnant again, and her husband was captured again. She lost her second child in the eighth month of her pregnancy.

In April 1943 soldiers came to Toby's house and demanded that all present go to the synagogue. Toby pleaded with the soldiers to let her stay and care for her sick child, but she was beaten and they were forced to leave. Two days later she and her child were taken to the ghetto, where they remained with her grandmother and aunt. Toby struggled to survive within the ghetto with no money and very little food. One day, a friend snuck out with her own jewelry as well as Toby's, intending to hide it in her basement so it could be reclaimed when they returned. After the war, Toby was unable to find it because her friend, who had died in Auschwitz, had not told her where she'd hidden it.

The SS liquidated the ghetto in March 1944 and sent Toby to Auschwitz with her mother, two brothers, three-year-old child and three cousins. Upon arrival, a man took Toby aside and told her to give her child to an older woman. A second man also told Toby to give her child to an older woman as their line neared Mengele, who was making the selections. "I used to live with my mother, so I give the baby . . . to my mother. And I hear right now how he cried, 'Mommy, I want to go with you. I want to stay with Mommy.' So I was by Mengele, and he told me I should go this side. My mother with my child the other side." Upon hearing her child screaming, she ran after her mother and child, but they had disappeared. She was reassured that they would soon be reunited. "They told us we gonna work, and all the people with children and they go . . . you know, they're going to mind the children, and we're gonna come every Sunday to see them. (Crying) But that Sunday never came."

Toby was taken to Lager C and remained there for three months. Her cousin constantly told her to eat to survive so they could remain together. Her cousin refused to allow Toby to give up hope and encouraged her to maintain her strength and will to live. At Lager B, where she was transferred, Toby noticed family camps where children were with their parents. One night she was awakened by screaming and discovered that everyone in the family camp had been selected for extermination in the crematorium.

Toby was told once again by friends that the children were being protected and that no harm would come to her child. "We wanted they should live. . . . For six months we didn't know what to think. We saw. We heard. We knew everything, but we didn't believe it. We didn't want to take it in our heads."

Toby was chosen during a selection and taken to the showers. Unsure if water or gas would come from the faucets, the group survived and was placed in a forced labor group. Toby was placed in the camp's tailor shop, where she made uniforms. Every four weeks, the workers were taken to the baths, disinfected and given new clothes. Toby recalled an occasion when no clothes were given to them and she returned to her barrack naked, with only a blanket.

Toby remembered, "I wanted to survive. I wanted to see my baby. I wanted to see my husband. And I tried. . . . Every four weeks they made selections. Mengele came in, and we had to strip all our clothes . . . when you had anything on your body, a little pimple, you went in the left side . . . they didn't know they went to the gas chamber."

Life and death blended together, but Toby struggled to survive so she could determine the fate of her child. Nine months after her arrival, Toby spoke to a man who laughed at her and called her a "dumb Hungarian." He continued laughing and told Toby she was ridiculous to believe that the Germans would feed Jewish children who might grow up to have other Jewish children after the war. Toby was informed that her child had been killed the day she arrived in Auschwitz. "Don't you see the fire? Don't you smell the . . . the smell? What do you think is there? This is your children. This is your parents."

Toby remained in Auschwitz for nine months. On January 18, 1945, she was forced into a death march from Auschwitz to Ravensbruck. She remembered that half of those forced on the march did not survive it. She survived with her cousin and was in Ravensbruck for four weeks, when SS soldiers forced her and her friends to work for them. Toby stole food from the soldiers and fed some of the sick and weaker people within the camp.

After a few months in Ravensbruck, Toby was transported to Mauthausen, where she remained until her liberation by the Americans on May 5, 1945. When she returned to Romania, she learned that all her brothers had survived and that her husband had died. Toby learned that only fifty out of five thousand in her hometown had survived the Holocaust.

In 1947 Toby married a fellow survivor and the couple moved to Germany, then Paris, and back to Germany. Toby and her husband emigrated to the United States in 1950, joining two of her older brothers.

Toby and her husband, Ephram, purchased a butcher shop and raised five children who gave them fifteen grandchildren. The couple lives in New York half the year and in Florida the remainder of the year. Both are very active and have recently celebrated their fiftieth wedding anniversary.

HOW TOBY S. COPED

Toby survived by utilizing emotion-focused coping strategies that centered around her will to be reunited with her child and other family members. With the encouragement of her friends and cousin, she continued to survive, despite her weakened condition. The affiliations with and support of others within the camp were vital to her survival.

It is clear that Toby also utilized the emotion-focused coping strategies of denial and intellectualization during her internment in Auschwitz. Numb to the reality of her child's death, despite witnessing the extermination of others, the selections, the flames and the smell, she continued to believe that her child was alive and well.

During her internment after the forced march from Auschwitz, Toby's affiliation with others was important to her survival. She reported that she also assisted others to survive by stealing food for them.

PHONE INTERVIEW WITH TOBY S.

Toby reported that she survived because of her hope for reunion with her child and her husband. She talked about her child being separated from her at the gates of Auschwitz and her mother taking her infant child from her arms. Toby said that the soldiers had promised they would be reunited and that the older people were caring for the infants in another part of the complex. She wanted to believe their deceptions. "They told us every Sunday that we would see the children . . . we hoped for six months." While sobbing, she recounted, "We didn't know . . . we wanted to believe."

Denial was a powerful coping tool, which helped her believe that human beings would not kill innocent infants and children. She stated that inmates knew people were being burned in the crematorium, but she and other mothers who had lost their children hoped that they were burning those who had died, not living infants and children.

Toby also stated that she did not care about living without her child. "I didn't want to eat." Toby stated that her cousin noticed she was not eating and forced her to resume. "She said we gonna eat together . . . she saved me."

Clearly, Toby's coping and survival were based on her affiliations with those who assisted her survival, as well as the hope of reunion with her child and family.

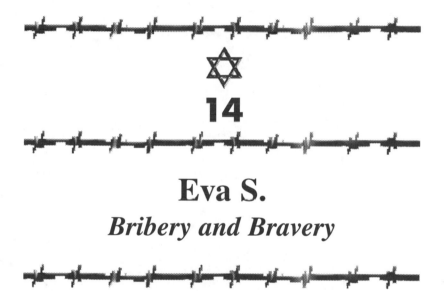

14

Eva S.
Bribery and Bravery

va S. was born on January 15, 1919, in Kozienice, Poland. She was one of five children raised in a middle-class family. As the oldest, she was often responsible for her younger siblings. Eva's father sold leather and, because of his travels to Radom, in 1933 he heard of the Nazis' rising power.

"We would read the paper. We knew it's going to come, something. Just nobody believed, nobody believed." Eva's family was aware of Kristallnacht, the destruction of Jewish property and synagogues, and the treatment of fellow Jews in other areas of the country. The families in the community mistakenly concluded that because they were law-abiding they would not be punished or scapegoated.

Occupation of Poland was complete within eight days in September 1939. On the first day of bombing, Eva and her family ran for safety into the woods surrounding Kozienice. The family was captured and returned to the city within twenty-four hours. The Nazis collected all the Jews and placed them in a ghetto within the city. The SS beat many of the men and placed them in a concentration camp near Radom and captured and forced others to work on digging patrols in nearby communities. Many of the men who remained were old and unable to resist, while other men were psychologically beaten into subservience. The SS left the women and children living in the ghettos.

"We were already very scared. . . . We were a middle-class family . . . and we stopped living. We had to fight for every day, to get the food on the table." Each day became a struggle subject to curfew. Though at first Eva and her family believed that the persecution would not continue, eventually the atrocities and their likely fate overwhelmed them.

Eva's family was aware of plans scheduled by the SS to

liquidate the ghetto in October 1940. Eva feared being separated from her parents, so she bribed an official to have her family's names placed on a list of Jews being transported to Sharzysko to dig ditches. Eva reported, "I was ready to do everything for . . . my sister or brothers to live, even get shot. It didn't bother me."

Eva bribed the Kapos and German officers to move her family to Szydlowiec and later to Pionki, where the family worked in an ammunition factory for two years. Life in Pionki was difficult but the family survived, believing that things would be all right as long as they remained together.

"Like I say, my life wasn't worth anything with that. . . . Just we were together still, (the remaining) four of us. And this gave us some kind of . . . you know . . . we're going to make it. . . . Was every day struggle. People were good one to each other, one to another. I think we helped one another however much we could under these circumstances."

In 1943 the Allies began bombing Pionki, and the transport from the concentration camp began late that year. The SS transported Eva and her mother and sister to Auschwitz. They deported her father and brother to Mauthausen and shot them on April 28, 1945, while on a death march.

Upon arrival in Auschwitz, Eva, her mother and sister were placed in lines for selection. They were spared when the gas chambers did not work. "We were taken . . . and we were sitting there . . . and we were like already dead people. We didn't care so much about life anyway. We was just sitting and waiting; and one person said, 'Oh, they going to gas us.' And one person said, 'Oh, what you talking about?' Was like no interest in life anymore. Was like, really, we got to a point that's what they did to us all the time . . . we got to a point we didn't care anymore. How much can a person take? You see, it was every time somebody you love so much you see taken away . . . your father, your brother, you know. I was happy I still had my little sister near me and my mother."

Eva, her mother, her sister and, later, her aunt were transported from Auschwitz to the Birkenau camp for two or three months. "I was begging to see an airplane bombing us. 'God please . . . let be finish.' We couldn't go . . . restroom, just once a day they took us. Every day . . . the Kapos said, 'Today you're going to go to the ovens.' You hear the nicest music, Beethoven, playing; and we didn't know then that a group of people were going to the oven. . . . We could smell . . . the burning, the flesh."

On one occasion the Gestapo came into the concentration camp and wanted to take Eva's sister, five other young children and a pregnant woman back to Auschwitz. Eva tried to remain with her little sister and protect her by telling the Gestapo soldier she was also pregnant. The SS soldier, enraged, took a shovel and beat Eva until she could not walk. "I knew I'm going to come back and my sister is not going to be anymore." Knowing that she might never see her sister again, she went to a camp engineer's office and attempted bribing him with a diamond ring to save her sister. The engineer said, "If you're going to bribe me, if you are thinking I am a person like this . . . I'm not going to help you." Three hours later a German officer came to Eva and said, "I want to help you. And I can help you. Just tell me what's going on." Crying so hard she could barely speak, Eva told the officer of the fate of her sister and the five young children. Later that day Eva discovered that he, indeed, did save the six children from transport back to Auschwitz.

The group was transferred from Auschwitz to Bergen-Belsen and then to Elsnig, a subcamp of Buchenwald. The Russians liberated Eva, her mother and sister in May 1945, after Italians aided the women while hiding in the woods. Eva returned to Krozienice to look for her family. Eva's mother, sister, three aunts and three cousins survived the Holocaust. She learned later that only forty or fifty people from her hometown of Kozienice had survived.

Eva then went to Lodz, Poland, to find her best friend, after hearing she had survived the war. In Lodz she met and married her husband, Henry, also a survivor. In 1949 Eva, Henry, and their first child emigrated to Israel, and in 1959 they emigrated to the United States.

Eva and Henry had two children and four grandchildren. Both Eva and Henry were very active in business. Henry died in 1972. Eva currently lives in Maryland and is active in her community.

HOW EVA S. COPED

Eva exhibited a combination of coping strategies for survival during the Holocaust. During the pre-camp experiences, as well as during internment in Auschwitz and other camps, Eva illustrated the importance of affiliation with others, an emotion-focused coping strategy. She maintained her efforts to create any means possible to keep her family together. On numerous occasions she bribed and pleaded with officials to keep her family safe from harm and remain a solidified group. While coping with the atrocities, she reported that she found herself emotionally numb, but she continued to find opportunities to use problem-focused coping mechanisms if openings arose to manipulate the environment. On many occasions, Eva placed herself in very risky and dangerous situations to save herself, her family and others in need.

Eva reported that she smuggled extra food she obtained from a female Gestapo officer to share with her family and others in need. "I always risked my life. I didn't care so much." The fact that she maintained hope that her family would survive the atrocities suggests emotion-focused coping strategies. Eva remembered, "We couldn't think anymore, I think, to a point. And not care. Just still care about the family; the family was mine (life)."

Luck also appeared to play a large part in Eva's report, as illustrated in her escape from the gas chambers. Being saved from the liquidation was an unimaginable destiny.

PHONE INTERVIEW WITH EVA S.

Eva could not explain the reason for her survival. "To be honest with you, there is no explanation for surviving." Eva stated it is impossible to understand how they were taken to the gas chambers and then let out. She stated that perhaps some of her survival had to do with luck.

Eva's family was most important to her. She told a story of how she attacked a Blockälteste who was harming her mother. Eva was not killed for the action, and that was unexplainable to her. She also told a story of a Mengele selection in Auschwitz, during which she was to be separated from her mother and sister. She bribed a German woman and was allowed to take her sister's and mother's hands and walk them over to the "line of life," while the German woman pretended to look the other way.

Eva was obviously concerned with the safety of her sister and her mother, and was willing to do whatever was necessary to protect them from harm. "I knew that I didn't want to live without my family." The incident of her brave act to save her sister from being transported back to Auschwitz illustrated that Eva was willing to protect her family at all cost.

15

Magda B.
Assistance and Resistance

agda B. was born on August 19, 1916, in Michalkovice, Slovakia (Austria-Hungary). Magda remembered a very happy childhood as the only daughter of five children. As a young child, she was very athletic and skinny. Her father was a Jewish-history teacher, and her mother instilled in her the values of caring for others, especially the poor and others in need.

Magda was always willing to give up her food so that others might have it for the Sabbath. "I grew up helping people and helping neighbors. I always said I will be a doctor because this is also helping the children."

In her early teens Magda established a kindergarten where she could care for young children within her community. She was once detained to be sent to a factory in Bata but was given exception papers because she was a teacher. However, a few days later, in the summer of 1942, Magda was deported in a crowded cattle car heading to Auschwitz.

Upon arrival in Auschwitz, the deportees were immediately placed in a barrack, where German female prisoners warned them that the tea being distributed was poisoned. "So here we were dehydrated and hungry, and we didn't know what to do. So I volunteered. I said, 'Listen, girls, we have to do something. We can't last so. We are dried out.'" Magda tested the drink to protect the other women and determined the tea was untainted. During processing, Magda helped other women who were collapsing from the cold. After being shaved, she was tattooed with the number 2318. All the women were disinfected and placed ten at a time in large bins of murky water. "Naked, wet, we stood that freezing cold wintry day until we got the remnants of Russian prisoner-of-war uniforms, which were cotton top and cotton pants."

The group of approximately six hundred women were the charge of a female German political prisoner. To gain respect from the German woman, Magda offered to help bring drinks to the prisoners. Magda carried the heavy containers to the barrack to prove her strength and competence. This helped her gain the acceptance of the German woman, who later protected her and arranged for Magda to work inside scrubbing floors. Magda argued with the German woman that it would be better if she worked outside so she could condition herself to the environment of Auschwitz. The German woman insisted that Magda would not last three days working outdoors and told her that she must help her clean the floors. Magda never again volunteered to work in the fields, and later she helped deliver food.

During her early years in Auschwitz, Magda encouraged others to organize and steal food, medications and rags. She used these materials to aid others in need. Even when hungry, she often gave her ration of food to others. Magda was once confronted by a woman who told her, "Enough is enough. Now you are going to sit down and have your meal." Magda said, "That's where it started, and together we had to help each other."

The beatings, the malnutrition and the unsanitary conditions took the lives of many young women. In August 1942 the group of surviving women was taken from Auschwitz to Birkenau. "If Auschwitz was hell, then Birkenau was (where) Satan exists." The sanitary and living conditions were much worse than at Auschwitz, and the women were tortured sadistically. "There was a barrack from clay, which meant before it was for horses. And the place for one horse suddenly became lodging for thirty women . . . they could lie like sardines, covered up with one blanket. . . . You couldn't go properly to the toilet. There was just a hole, and over a hole a piece of plank, and you was sitting on the plank . . . with lots of people . . . and if you fell in, that was the finish."

Magda remembered her dedication to living through the atrocities of Birkenau and thinking, "Every day when you are alive . . . maybe there will be a chance that something will happen and prolong the life. Maybe some miracle will happen and the war will come to the end, and then we will recuperate."

On one occasion, Magda was selected to be taken to the gas chamber. The German woman for whom she had worked in the barracks pulled her from the truck that took the other women to the gas chamber. Magda reported that the female Kapo tricked the SS guard in charge, grabbed her from the truck headed to the crematorium and told her to run.

On another occasion, all the women in Magda's barrack were going to be sent to the gas chambers because they had been tearing their blankets to pad parts of their bodies for protection from the cold. Magda reported that she stepped forward and told the commanders, "If you were in the same position as we are, you would do the same thing to survive." The SS guard began to scream at Magda for her insolence, but, amused by her antics, the commander gave the group new clothes and saved them from death. "And this is what we did, how we helped each other."

Other non-Jewish prisoners helped the Jewish women. Magda remembered a woman who was maintaining the written record (Reportschreiberin) as a selection was being made. When the SS man left, "She sends the girls back to the barracks. And so she saved about three hundred girls from immediate death. How long they will be alive, this nobody could guarantee." It was later discovered that the woman had written down numbers of people who had already perished, and this trickery assisted hundreds to escape extermination. Magda reported that this type of diversion from death was accomplished through courage and trickery. "We are just going once through the chimney, sooner or later. But till we arrive, we have to help each other. And that's how we helped each other."

Magda's testimony revealed numerous examples of assisting others in need, as well as other women assisting Magda. When Magda came down with typhoid, the women protected her by bribing the German woman in charge of the barracks. Promising that they would look after Magda, the women carried her out to work. Upon their return one day from the work detail, her friends protected Magda from a selection by holding her up and placing her between women who were healthy. "Luckily, the girls on both sides who carried me, they were in better shape so they didn't see me in between. Which saved me."

Magda's personal mission was to minimize suffering by manipulating the environment for other women whenever possible. If nothing could be accomplished in a physical fashion, Magda was determined to be a source of support and encouragement as well as a calming force. To save as many women as possible, she attempted to trick the SS during selection by placing weaker women in the middle of rows to prevent them from being noticed.

"So I arranged the girls so that in the front and in the back was a strong girl . . . and in the middle was the weaker ones. And I pushed the girls together." Confronted by an SS guard about her scheme, Magda used her intellectual creativity to create a diversion for the situation, promising that these weaker women could be useful to Germany by assisting in the "recycling" of clothes. Magda suggested that the women could wash and repair clothes, and she guaranteed that she would produce favorable results if the women were allowed to live.

During her internment in Auschwitz-Birkenau, Magda was made the assistant to the Blockälteste. Magda kept busy trying to obtain more food for everyone and to help them survive. In 1943 she was named the block supervisor of Barrack 10, which was used for medical experiments. She became the protégé of Hauptsturmführer Dr. Edward Wirths, who was in charge of all medical personnel at KL (Konzentrationslager) Auschwitz. Magda offered psychological support and encouragement to the women in the experimental barrack. "I tried to help them . . . because either you try your best or you don't care. But I cared. Wherever I could, I helped."

Magda spoke of her relationship with Irma Grese, the female SS guard called the "Angel of Death." Magda reported that she met Grese in August 1942 in the early days of internment in Auschwitz. "I was a Stubendienst—a helper . . . just like a little helper who . . . carried the bread and the food. . . . She was in charge as an SS woman." Grese reportedly noticed that Magda was different from the other women. Grese asked her name, and Magda informed her that she would encourage the women until her last breath. Magda reported that she accompanied Grese on numerous occasions to meet some of the women Grese had raped and continued to use for her sexual gratification. Magda was many times used as a diversion, as well as someone Grese asked about her choice of women.

As the years passed, Grese became more powerful in the SS system, and the record of her brutality to female prisoners also grew. Known for her cruelty, raping, torturing with whips and other acts of sadism, Grese was feared by everyone in the camp. All knew of her brutality. Magda remembered, "This was Grese. She could talk to me . . . like a friend; and the next minute she was a devil . . . that's what she was. A real devil. A sadistic devil.

But she was so pretty, you know? That's why they called her 'Angel of Death.'"

Magda was later made camp commander of the Hungarian Jews being transported to Birkenau from Budapest. In the summer of 1942, she was named Lagerälteste under Kommandant Josef Kramer. The Hungarian transports arrived from May through December of that year. Unafraid to speak her mind, Magda told Kramer that if she was to be Lagerältester she had to have supplies, such as blankets, straw, utensils and spoons. Magda told Kramer that she needed thirty women, whom she must choose, to assist her with the Hungarian arrivals. She demanded that the thirty women be chosen to assist other prisoners as much as possible. "So again, miracle of miracles, they thought—you know, the news traveled—that I am the protégé of Kramer. . . . I just couldn't save everybody."

During her final year in the camps, Magda was given a job counting potatoes in the Lager kitchen, and later she was named a camp supervisor of Russian prisoners in a fabric-production facility. On January 18, 1945, she and others were forced on a death march to Malchow, the subcamp of Ravensbruck located near Mecklenburg. After noticing that those who lagged toward the back were at greater risk of being shot, Magda gathered prisoners and moved them up front to escape death. She and the other survivors were liberated by the Soviet army.

After the war, Magda returned to her hometown and discovered that three of her brothers had survived the Shoah. She also learned that two of her brothers had been partisans.

Magda left her hometown and moved to Prague, where she met her husband, Bela, another survivor who had lost his wife and child in the Holocaust. The couple married in 1946 and settled in Bohemia, but the Communists took over the area in

1948. Bela refused to join the Communist party and was expelled. The Communists took away the couple's business and their house. Magda and Bela then emigrated to Israel penniless. Magda worked there as a kindergarten teacher.

In 1965 Magda, her husband, and their two children settled in Australia. The couple purchased a small business and had two children and four grandchildren. They stay very active in Australia. Magda has been interviewed many times and continues to teach others about the lessons of the Holocaust. She has been interviewed by the Spielberg Foundation and has also been interviewed for a documentary to be shown in Australia. In 1952 fellow Auschwitz survivor and physician Dr. Gisella Perl, a Jewish physician Magda knew in Auschwitz, wrote an article about Magda.

HOW MAGDA B. COPED

Magda utilized both emotion-focused and problem-focused coping mechanisms. She constantly surveyed her environment for opportunities to manipulate and create options, and she found many ways of organizing situations for survival. Despite the risk to her own well-being and safety, she stood up for herself and others and her resistance created many opportunities to bring about needed change. Her determination, will to survive and morale-boosting personality were valuable sources of encouragement and support.

Magda grasped the realities of her environment and was willing to watch for ways she could help herself and others survive. With great strength and determination, she stood up to many SS guards and commanders in order to negotiate options for survival.

She learned during her childhood, from her mother, about protecting others. She demonstrated this attribute many times, and many others assisted her in her times of need. Magda was concerned with others' survival and told them, "Life here is not a pleasure. But I am going to try to make your life as easy as possible, with your help. We have to communicate. We have to manage to help each other because typhus is raging." She was determined to save as many lives as possible during her internment in the camp.

Her leadership capabilities and strong will illustrated Magda's abilities to create opportunities for survival in an environment filled with horrors and brutality, trauma and death. By encouraging others to retain their hope, Magda established what Viktor Frankl described as a "meaning" or "purpose" to survive within the massive traumatization of Auschwitz.

PHONE INTERVIEW WITH MAGDA B.

Magda emphasized that Auschwitz was a horrible experience and that she had no special technique for survival, except the will to keep others alive. "It was such a hard life . . . you couldn't describe it if I told you for hours. . . . How can you put three and a half years in a talk?" In her opinion, perseverance, commitment and split-second decisions were factors that determined life and death.

Magda's entire life was filled with the purpose of serving others. "I tried to help wherever I could." She tried to encourage others, and many were willing to listen to her. Many others also cared for her safety and survival. She was saved by others on many occasions, including the times she was taken by a German woman from the truck being sent to the crematorium, saved from death by her friends when she had typhus and aided by men within the camp who respected her for her taking charge and caring for others.

Magda was determined to risk all to help others because, "We go only once through the chimney." She was very active in organizing the prisoners and was willing to risk her life for others— and they were willing to do the same for her.

Through the Eyes of Magda B.

So I turn to you, all parents, to all the teachers, professors, scientists, preachers, priests, rabbis. Educate the children, the people, about the horrors that the German nation under the Nazi system did to all other nations, not only Jews. . . . And who, for a lot of money, tried to persuade the world about the nonexistence of the gas chambers. But would you . . . forget it, if you would live through all the horrors which changed your life, your career? We're tormented by nightmares. When we close our eyes, we relive the misery again and again. So we don't even go to sleep. And how about the millions and millions of babies, young, innocent children, people young and old? So please! Don't minimize the Holocaust as an old story. But try to work against it, that happenings like the Holocaust shouldn't have grounds to happen again, ever!

. . . People should be vigilant all the time not to, not to think that this really doesn't matter. All these . . . hate mongers that come up in the world and people, if they're not personally marked, they think that it's nothing. It will pass by. It will blow away. But, if you let it go, (get) out of hand, then this, this can happen (again).

16

Helen W.
A Daily Dose of Dignity

elen W. was born on April 14, 1909, in a small town across the river from Frankfurt-on-Rhine, Germany. Her family was not very religious but attended synagogue services on Rosh Hashanah and Yom Kippur. Helen's mother was of German descent, and her father was born in Lithuania. In 1914 during World War I, the family "became all of a sudden Russians because Lithuania belonged to Russia at the time. And as Russians, we were the enemies of Germany, and we would have been interned if we couldn't live with my maternal grandparents, who at this time came from a very small town in Germany." Because of her father's ancestry, the family did not register at the police station, a choice that forced the family to live underground. Though unable to attend a public school, Helen attended a liberal Jewish school to which she was admitted without a birth certificate. She continued her education there until she was eighteen years old.

Helen did not view the world during her childhood as Jewish and non-Jewish. "In some way I was not aware that the children I was playing with on the streets were neighbors who were not Jewish, because all the children I knew were Jewish. . . . I was thinking I was living in a Jewish world."

Helen was able to support herself financially, assist her family, and take vacations on a nearby island, Norderney, which was limited to Jews. Here she met her husband, Siegfried, who was quite persistent in pursuing her. They married in 1933, and in 1934 they moved to Amsterdam.

Many other Jews chose to leave Germany during those years and emigrated to surrounding countries, such as Holland, which would accept Jews. Helen was active in assisting others who needed to find housing and assistance in Amsterdam. She also worked as an interior decorator, adding to the family income.

While living in Holland in 1937, she gave birth to her only daughter, Doris. In November 1938, at the time of Kristallnacht, she heard that her father and brother had been arrested in Frankfurt. Luckily, however, before the invasion of Holland, her brother, father and mother were able to emigrate to the United States.

The Nazis invaded and occupied Holland in May 1940. Two years later, the Nazis ordered Helen, Siegfried and their daughter to appear with one suitcase each at the train station in Amsterdam.

"We didn't understand what really would happen to us. All our friends came and we gathered in the house and talked. . . . We all had come from Germany, and each of us had a little girl about the same age. . . . And . . . my husband and I, we decided we go to the Jewish Council."

The Jewish Council told them that they would be sent to a family camp to work and that someone would care for the children while the parents were in forced-work camps. "We left this building and I decided to tell my husband that I am not going on July 15 to get that train. And we, being brought up in Germany, which is a little different than other countries . . . had a hard time to accept that. . . . Who knows what they will do to us if we don't go? Who knows what they do to us when we are going?" After deciding to delay their transport, the couple found a surgeon who agreed to take out Siegfried's appendix (which was healthy) in an attempt to delay their departure until the next order was given. During this time, the Nazis forced Jews to wear yellow Stars of David, limited them to purchasing food and necessities during certain daytime hours, and forbid them to be on any street at night.

In early October 1942, a friend told Helen that they could be assisted in living underground and that their child could be sent to a safe location. The rescuers (Joe Vis and his wife Agaat), who were non-Jews, aided by the members of a small liberal church, assisted the family with the plans. The rescuers didn't have much money, but they wanted to help us as much as they could. They told Helen, "We (do) not know how long the war will be. We have a place for a child if you want to give her up." The rescuers told Helen and Siegfried that they would hide Doris until the end of the war. Thus, Helen, Siegfried and Joe Vis arranged for five-year-old Doris to be housed with an anonymous family. "We did not know their name and we did not know where they were living," but they later learned it was Joe's sister's family.

The people from the church assisted the couple with plans for living underground. Helen noted that there were over twenty thousand people in hiding from the Germans in Holland. The couple lived underground from October 1942 to August 1944 "in different homes because people got very scared very often. Sometimes (they) wanted us to leave the same day. Some places (they lasted) two or three months until they got so scared." They hid for eleven months in Haarlem while the Allies invaded France. They felt optimistic upon the liberation of Paris in August 1944 by the Allies. Unfortunately, on that same day, the Gestapo arrested Helen and Siegfried.

Helen reported that she and Siegfried were fully aware of the potential danger of their situation. They had remained informed of current events by listening to BBC radio transmissions, so she was quite sure they would be transported to Auschwitz. The Gestapo told Helen, who was standing next to a child, "'If this is your child and if you have more children in hiding, we recommend that you take them with you because you are going into a family camp. . . . And . . . they will be taken care of while you are working. . . .' We went completely without luggage, knowing that we probably would come to Auschwitz because this was in some way called a punishment that we did not follow the first time . . . that we had to be punished for that, so it could only have been Auschwitz." After two straight days of Gestapo interrogation concerning the underground network, Helen was transported to Westerbork and then to Auschwitz-Birkenau in 1944.

The train ride was a nightmare. On the overloaded cattle cars, Helen and her traveling companions had nowhere to sit, no food or water, no light and no toilet facilities. SS soldiers came onboard during stops and forced the prisoners to give all of their belongings to them. As an act of resistance, Siegfried ripped up all his money so that the SS would never take anything from them.

Helen remembered the ramp at her arrival point in Auschwitz, which appeared to go on forever. The women were separated from the men. Siegfried was directed to one location and Helen to another. "It seemed endless, and there was a man standing who made the decision who shall live or who shall die, but we did not know that." The man on the ramp was Dr. Mengele. "He sent me, it was the side of life, and the other was the side of death, as I heard the next day also. And . . . there were no Jewish children in Auschwitz, just a few Dr. Mengele wanted."

Helen told of a woman who allowed herself to be separated from her children, knowing that she could not help them. The woman knew that she would be killed if she stayed with her children and she made the "choiceless choice" to allow her children to be taken away. Helen spoke of the difficulty of living with such a decision. "The woman said to me, 'You know what I did? I knew they would kill the children, and I let my children go.' I don't know how she lived through it. . . . How do you live with that? I wish she was living and could have children again."

Helen told of the tattooing, of being stripped naked and of having all her body hair shaved during processing. "Probably the most upsetting was this being changed into a different person with losing your hair, losing everything you had, just as you are born. I think that was the greatest shock. You couldn't see yourself, but you saw others, so you knew what you were looking like. I think it was the greatest shock for all of us because nobody menstruated anymore. That was over."

Sleep was almost impossible with ten to twelve women crowded into one bunk, and early morning brought roll call. The number of people in attendance never matched the number in the books. Helen remembered that many of the Polish women appeared stronger than the Western European Jews. Perhaps many of the Polish women had been conditioned and numbed to the horrors from being in other camps and ghettos between 1939 and 1944. Many of the Poles appeared to help each other. Helen made a friend, a Hungarian, who was a keeper of the latrine and washroom.

Helen was determined to wash every day to maintain her dignity. She was able to do so by sneaking into the washroom on a regular basis, assisted by her Hungarian friend. "But it gave me a very good feeling that I had done that. . . . The friendship I had with . . . the woman from Hungary helped me to get in and have some time to talk to her. . . . I could always get in. And . . . we became good friends." The support she gained from her friendship and maintenance of dignity was essential to her survival.

Helen remembered that Anne Frank, her sister Margot and her mother were on the transport to Auschwitz with them. She knew the Franks in Holland, and she remembered that Mr. Frank was a very intelligent man. Anne appeared to be closer to her father than to her mother. She seemed a very shy and quiet girl and was not as pretty as her sister. She learned years later that the Frank sisters died in Bergen-Belsen shortly before liberation.

Helen remained interned in Birkenau until October 28, 1944, when she was transported to work in the Kratzau factory in Czechoslovakia. "They didn't tell us it was Czechoslovakia. It was high up in the mountains . . . was nice, and it was a good feeling to be away from those killing places and from the chimney." Female SS guards secured the camp and its twelve hundred female prisoners. Helen reported that Kratzau had no running water, that it was never possible to wash and that everyone was quickly full of lice. The workday lasted twelve hours, and the factory had a day shift and a night shift. Those who chose the night shift were allowed an extra portion of food. Barely sheltered, without blankets or heat, most women barely survived the cold winter, and many did not. As the war continued, rations were cut. "We were on our way down physically, but when the International Red Cross came actually into the camp . . . there were four women coming in green uniforms, and we were standing in our five lines, and I heard the commandant in German tell them, 'You just saw our beautiful shower installations. Look at those filthy Jews. They do not want to wash themselves. Those pigs.' And . . . none of those women asked . . . why we didn't want to wash." Helen supplied the answer: There was no water.

Near the end of the war, Helen was taken to the POW camp where she was liberated and told to wait for the arrival of the International Red Cross. Helen refused to wait and traveled to a displaced persons' (DP) camp in Pilsen.

Upon her return to Holland, Helen reunited with her daughter Doris. Siegfried never returned. They assumed he had died in Auschwitz. "I never have seen him again and . . . there is no record for the dead. There's a record of the trains . . . the numbers of the trains and how many people were in the trains . . . but they have no record of who died."

Helen recounted the difficulties of reuniting with her daughter. The little eight-year-old girl appeared scared when Helen arrived where she was living. "I didn't come close to her. I didn't touch her. . . . We had nothing. We had no bed. Nothing. I . . . felt I needed her. I needed her very much. We need our children more than they need us. That's something I learned." Friends assisted Helen and Doris by giving them a place to sleep. In 1947 mother and daughter emigrated to their family in the United States.

HOW HELEN W. COPED

Helen's testimony depicted her utilization of problem-focused coping skills during her years in hiding and during the postwar occupation. Helen and her family appeared at those times to experience more freedom and opportunity to manipulate and cope with the environment through problem-solving strategies. The opportunity to save her child by giving her to a stranger must have involved a substantial, if not an extreme, amount of emotion-focused coping, but Helen never mentioned that. She did, however, comment that she had great difficulty with emotion-focused coping during internment. Helen's memories of trigger events, such as children being ripped from their mothers' arms, children being sent to "family camps" with their parents, and seeing no children in Auschwitz except those "used" by Mengele for his own purposes, correlate to the pain she felt upon losing her child.

Helen coped by using hope and her intellect. She described a conversation she overheard between SS guards as they marched to the working camp: "You see . . . when we marched to the factory, (I was) always in the last row . . . there were two soldiers with us and they spoke German. I could hear what they were saying to each other. And it was . . . music in my ears, because they said they were terribly upset. They hadn't heard for weeks from their families, and they said that Germany is bombed and then all of a sudden I heard that the Allies are in Nuremberg. And I thought, in Nuremberg . . . in the middle of the country. And I told my friends and I said, oh that cannot take long at all anymore. That must be over soon. They are already in Nuremberg. But we were the ones who really suffered so much because it was so cold and we had so little strength left. We buried our women that died. We didn't know the names. We . . . we had no strength anymore to discuss, to talk, which we did in the beginning."

Helen commented that she had difficulty after the war reuniting with her daughter Doris, now nearing eight years of age, who had been in hiding in Amsterdam. She suffered post-traumatic stress disorder due to massive traumatization, and she felt great pain and confusion at the time of reunion.

"I don't think that I was aware of what I had done to take her out of this secure home in this life with a woman who wasn't completely stable. I'm convinced I was the only one who didn't know. But I'm convinced. . . . I was only looking for a place for us to live that we (would be) just like a family and that she would . . . be home and I'm the mother. But we never discussed it, practically all our lives. . . . Maybe when she was . . . still in Amsterdam, one day she did something which I said she shouldn't. She said, I wish you wouldn't have come back."

Helen's concluding remarks provide valuable insight into the struggle and pain of survivors and their children. After reading a book called *I Never Said Good-Bye,* Helen told her daughter,

"I'm . . . very much upset that all those people who say they were abandoned say that still after they have children themselves. Don't they want to protect their children?" Her daughter reportedly stated, "No . . . I can understand. I wasn't abandoned." Helen continued, "It was the first time, and I said I will never learn that and never accept it. She went to New York then and she found the book and she sent it to me and she put in there, 'Thank you for giving me life twice.' It wasn't necessary to discuss it. Really. It would have made our relationship painful if we would have discussed it. If I would have constantly heard (from her that) I see it . . . the wrong way, then I never could (heal). So . . . she has understood after all those years."

APPENDIX A: THE FINDINGS

Appendix A contains statistical evidence that addresses the unique and resilient "voices" of women who experienced the horrors of Auschwitz. Within the following pages, you will find more documentation of the powerful impact of affiliation in women's survival. These "voices" create a new understanding of women's use of relational affiliation and emotional bonding as means of coping.

These statistical data summarize over one thousand pages of transcribed testimony provided by the sixteen survivors profiled in this book and produced by the United States Holocaust Memorial Museum (1988–1991), as well as more than twenty hours of taped telephone interviews from 1995.

The incidence and frequency of coping strategies noted by each survivor as part of their testimonies were recorded and calculated to validate the generalized conclusions of gender-specific adaptation in Auschwitz.

FINDINGS ON FEMALE COPING MECHANISMS

Table A.1 summarizes the frequency of those coping strategies used by women survivors (including emotional bonding and affiliation with other women) that were most frequently reported as the determining factor for survival for women in Auschwitz. Sustaining relationships, assisting a significant family member or friend, or the hope of being reunited with family or friends appeared in all of the testimonies. Clearly, the sixteen women's testimonies suggest the importance of maintaining emotional connections with others as a means of survival.

Of those who responded, 31 percent indicated that affiliation and emotional bonding were the most influential elements for their survival in Auschwitz. (The coping strategy of affiliation with other women is the composite of affiliation with others through maintenance of a relationship, 13.2 percent, and assistance from others, 18.1 percent.)

This sample of female Auschwitz survivors supports the prevailing trend in recent Holocaust studies and gender-related research that female survival, during massive traumatization, is enhanced and nourished by human connection. The results indicate that females tend to use gender-related coping and adaptation through their connections with others, which assists in their reconnection with their inner strength and purpose and meaning for survival.

These findings suggest that Holocaust scholars, such as Des Pres, Dimsdale, Eitinger, Frankl, Krystal and others, may lean toward a gender-biased male perspective. Therefore, a gender-neutral "blanket" interpretation of coping strategies for survival may not be accurate as it relates to male and female survivors of the Holocaust.

TABLE A.1: FEMALE SURVIVORS' INCIDENCE OF REPORTED COPING STRATEGIES

The raw data from the table can be converted to illustrate the incidence of reported female coping strategies by category.

Strategies	Mady D.	Fritzie F.	Alice C.	Nina K.	Ruth M.	Helen W.	Lily M.	Kate B.	Cecilie K.	Guta W.	Margaret K.	Barbara F.	Toby S.	Eva S.	Magda B.	Helen G.	Totals	
Personal Initiative		5	3		1	4	2		1						18	2	36	10.1%
Luck	1	1	2		2			1	3	3	1	1	1	1	1	1	19	5.4%
Technical Skills							1		1			1	1	1	2		5	1.4%
Appearance	1		1	1					1		1	1	1	1	1		9	2.5%
Relationships*			3		7	1	3	3	4	2			2	17	4		47	13.2%
Assist Others*	2	6	7	8	5	4	2	2	5	3			6		15	1	64	18.0%
Hope/ Reunion		1					2	1					4		1	1	10	2.8%
Organizing/ Resistance		1		2	4	1									9	1	18	5.1%
Faith			1	1	1	1		1				1			1	1	7	2.0%
Bear Witness		1		1	1	1	1			1						1	5	1.4%
Humor				1							11				1		3	0.8%
Will/ Meaning									1								1	0.3%
Total																	355	100%

* = The combination of relationships with others and assistance to others is categorized as affiliation with others (31.2%) of total occurrences.

TABLE A.1 (cont'd.): FEMALE SURVIVORS' INCIDENCE OF REPORTED COPING STRATEGIES

The raw data from the table can be converted to illustrate the incidence of reported female coping strategies by category.

Strategies	Mady D.	Fritzie F.	Alice C.	Nina K.	Ruth M.	Helen W.	Lily M.	Kate B.	Cecilie K.	Guta W.	Margaret K.	Barbara F.	Toby S.	Eva S.	Magda B.	Helen G.	Totals	
Task / Accplshmt															7		7	2.0%
Denial			1		1	2		1	2	1	2	3	3		6		22	6.2%
Personal Choice			1		1	2		1	2	1	2	3	3		6		22	6.2%
Rage							1		1						1		3	0.8%
Daily Task																	0	0.0%
ID w/ Aggressor															6		6	1.7%
Numb				2			1	1									4	1.1%
Depersonal																	0	0.0%
Hope		2	3	1	3	3		1	2				1		3	1	20	5.6%
Dignity					1						1		1		1	1	4	1.1%
Manipulate Environment	1		6		4	7	3		2		2	1	3	2	12		46	13.0%
Fantasy		2	1	2	2	1		1	1						1	1	8	2.3%
Total																	355	100%

* = The combination of relationships with others and assistance to others is categorized as affiliation with others (31.2%) of total occurrences.

TABLE A.2: INCIDENCE OF REPORTED FEMALE COPING STRATEGIES
A graphic bar chart relating to incidence in Table A.1

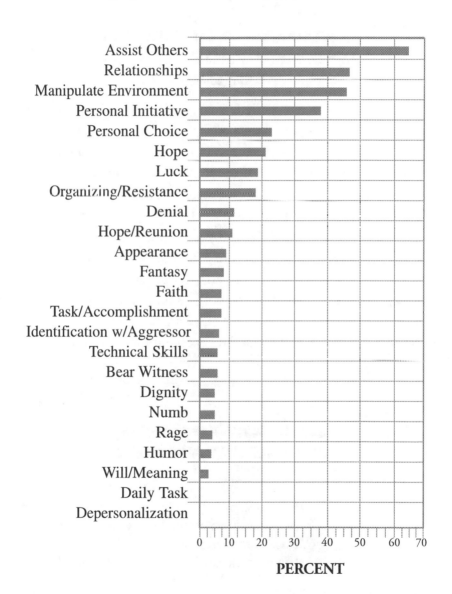

PERCENT

TABLE A.3: COMPARISON OF COPING STRATEGIES

RELATIONSHIP OF EMOTION-FOCUSED AND PROBLEM-FOCUSED COPING

The research data elicited from the sub-grouping suggest emotion-focused coping strategies (229 out of 355 occurrences or 64.5 percent) were used more often than those of problem-solving coping strategies (107 out of 355 occurrences or 30.1 percent). The results concur with the theoretical research of Lazarus and Folkman (1984), which suggested that emotion-focused coping strategies are primarily utilized in situations or events in which an individual realizes there is nothing that can be done to modify the threat, challenge or harm. As Lazarus and Folkman's theory suggested, emotion-focused strategies are appropriate when the individual believes that she cannot manipulate external factors in a fashion that would be beneficial for adaptation.

EMOTION-FOCUSED COPING STRATEGIES

Category	Coping Strategy	Occurrences	Total
Affiliation	A. Relationships	47	
	B. Assistance from others	64	
	C. Hope of reunion with family or friends	10	121/355

Category	Coping Strategy	Occurrences	Total
Theological or Philosophical	A. Faith/spiritual connection	7	
	B. Purpose or meaning/will to live	1	
	C. Goal of bearing witness	5	13/355
Psychological	A. Denial	11	
	B. Humor	3	
	C. Depersonalization	0	
	D. Numbing	4	
	E. Rage	3	
	F. Personal initiative	36	
	G. Hope	20	
	H. Fantasy	8	
	I. Identification	6	
	J. Maintenance of dignity	4	95/355

PROBLEM-FOCUSED COPING STRATEGIES

Category	Coping Strategy	Occurrences	Total
Active Behaviors	A. Technical skills	5	
	B. Tasks or accomplishments	7	
	C. Focus on daily tasks	0	
	D. Resistance or organizing	18	
	E. Manipulation of environment	46	
	F. Creating choices	22	
	G. Appearance	9	107/355

OTHER COPING STRATEGIES

Category	Occurrences	Total
Luck, Chance, Fate	19	19/355

The following figure illustrates the results as they relate to the frequency of the utilization of problem-focused versus emotion-focused coping, as well as the frequency of luck.

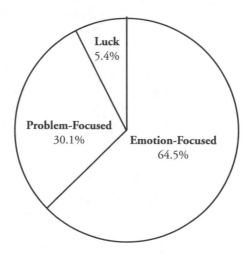

Percentage of Occurrences by Sub-Grouping Categories

The data suggest that problem-focused coping strategies were in force whenever the female survivors discovered an opportunity to create a change that might lend itself to the reduction of the threat, challenge or harm. Due to the massive traumatization, females in this population appeared to have little room for manipulation; but it was indicated that 43 percent of reported incidents (46 out of 107) utilized the active behaviors of problem-focused coping strategies. These techniques were used to alter the environment by manipulating externals. Examples of these behaviors include lying, creating diversions, bribing Kapos or Blockältestes, or any means to gain protection, exclusion from selections, or personal safety. Other examples of active problem-focused coping might involve creating diversions so that one prisoner could exchange places with another, lying about age, protection of a sister, mother or friend by physically supporting them during Appells, or performing labor for a weakened survivor.

The results concur with the findings of Benner, Roskies and Lazarus (1980), Cohen (1953), Kahana et al. (1988), and Lazarus (1966, 1978, 1984, 1991, 1993), which suggested that concentration-camp experiences differ from other massive traumatizations by limiting problem-focused coping strategies to minute manipulation of the environment. Limited manipulation of externals might include decisions such as whether to eat now or to eat later. The findings indicate that those experiencing extreme massive traumatization experience little choice in outcomes. Many of the female survivors indicated that they used a combination of both emotion-focused and problem-focused coping strategies when the environment allowed such means for adaptation and survival.

Comparing and contrasting the data collected from the telephone interviews with the survivors demonstrate that the survivors felt there was little opportunity to manipulate the environment. Survivors Mady D., Nina K. and Kate B. specifically stated there were no active strategies or "real" means with which to manipulate the environment. In fact, these three women began their telephone interviews by suggesting strongly that there were no techniques for survival. Despite the high incidence recorded in the oral testimonies of "manipulation of the environment," in the telephone interviews the survivors stated their beliefs that there were "no real choices" or means of altering the environment. This concurs with Benner, Roskies and Lazarus (1980), who contended that only minute manipulation of externals is possible during extreme massive traumatization, which places the "real choices" reported by the survivors in perspective.

To elicit their personal insights, interpretations and thoughts, fifty years after liberation, this author asked the survivors interviewed by telephone about their perceptions of coping strategies utilized in Auschwitz. The following table summarizes their responses, which are further explored in the individual text narratives.

TABLE A.4: COPING STRATEGIES REPORTED BY SURVIVORS

Survivor	Coping Strategy
Madeline (Mady) D.	"No technique or active strategy"
	Luck
	"Human drive to live"
	Assistance from others, encouragement
	Relationships with other women
	Hope of reunion with family
	Fantasy and dreaming
Nina K.	"No choices or ways to manipulate"
	"Live for one day, perhaps live to next day, and then the next day"
	Hope
	Dream and fantasize to regenerate

Survivor	Coping Strategy
Nina K. *(continued)*	Affiliation with others
	Luck and fate
Lily M.	Live one day at a time
	Desire to live
	Affiliation and relationships
	Assistance from others
	Time to be alone, dream, talk to G–d
	Caring for loved ones
Kate B.	No specific strategy for survival
	Fantasize about "old days"
	Fate
	Assistance from others
	"Optimistic viewpoint," hope
	Encouragement from others
	Self-esteem, a "confidence inside"
	Relationship with others
	Numbing
	Luck
Cecilie K.	"Desire to live, a will to live"
	Writing poetry

Survivor	Coping Strategy
Cecilie K. *(continued)*	Affiliation and relationships
	Luck and fate
	Concern for family members
Guta W.	Luck
	An "inner strength"
	Affiliation with other women
	Numbing
	Assistance from others
	Importance of family and protection
Margaret K.	Desire to live, "determination"
	Inner strength, "a tough cookie"
	Affiliation with others, friendship
	Assistance from others
	Numbing
Toby S.	Hope of seeing child once again
	Hope of seeing husband again
	Affiliation with others
	Assistance from others
	Denial of reality

Survivor	Coping Strategy
Eva S.	Can't explain, unsure of why I lived
	Luck, fate
	Affiliation with others, family
	Assistance from other women
Magda B.	No specific technique for survival
	Assistance from others
	Taught to help others
	Organizing and resistance
	"Do whatever I could do"

Note: Telephone results procured and transcribed 11/95–12/95.

The responses indicate that 5.4 percent of the survivors sampled noted luck or fate played a part in their survival. The results of this research concur with the work of Cohen (1953), Jackson (1993) and Kahana et al. (1988), which implied that luck and fate played a large part in survival. The predominance of the incidence of luck or fate was noted in four (40 percent) of the ten telephone interviews of the female survivors of Auschwitz. As Cecilie K. stated, "How else can you explain that we lived?"

APPENDIX B: COPING STRATEGIES IN TRAUMA

Appendix B provides a brief review of the literature that examines human coping strategies during massive traumatization. Understanding the nature of coping is essential to understanding peoples' unique adaptations during the Holocaust. While facing atrocities and horrors beyond comprehension, people fought to respond, to find meaning, purpose and the will to take another breath to live. Though this information is not essential to grasping the full scope of the survivors' stories, its inclusion in this book makes it available to readers who are interested in a somewhat more academic understanding of such experiences. In addition, the references chapter contains full source citations for all books cited in Love Carried Me Home.

COPING MECHANISMS

While it has been recognized that the definitions for the term "stress" are varied and complex, it is also true that the term "coping" has a variety of definitions and synonyms. Terms such as "adaptation," "coping mechanisms," "coping strategies," "defense mechanisms" and "coping styles" all appear in the literature, sometimes producing different meanings. Dimsdale (1978) suggested that many researchers use coping as part of a stimulus-response paradigm, but actually the verb "to cope" is derived from the French verb *couper,* which means "to strike."

From Dimsdale's point of view, coping involves the ability to remain flexible and maintain survival in the long term. Dimsdale (1980) also stated that coping is only considered successful if the person's self-esteem is maintained as well as continuity with the past and the future.

Monat and Lazarus (1991) defined "coping" as an individual's attempt to master the demands exacerbated by harm, threat or loss that people perceive (appraise) as drains on their resources. Kahana et al. (1988) defined automatic or familiar reactions as "adaptive behaviors" and believed that coping is an individual's effort to master a problem and that the coping response is utilized as a means of recreating homeostasis (balance) in the individual. Lazarus (1966, 1991, 1993; Lazarus and Folkman, 1984; Lazarus and Launier, 1978) proposed that coping is a process that includes the entire time period from moment of perceived stress through the duration of appraisal, including the adaptation by the individual.

EMOTION-FOCUSED AND PROBLEM-FOCUSED COPING

R. S. Lazarus (1991) stated that coping consists of cognitive and behavioral techniques that are utilized to manage internal and external demands upon a human being. As Lazarus and Folkman (1984) explained, coping may be utilized in two specific ways to directly or indirectly affect the appraisal of a situation or adaptation to a stressor. The two coping strategies are "problem-focused coping" and "emotion-focused coping." Problem-focused coping is action-centered while emotion-focused coping involves thinking (cognitive) strategies rather than action strategies.

Lazarus and Folkman also suggested that problem-focused and emotion-focused coping are utilized at differing degrees of stress. They suggested that at low degrees of stress these two forms of coping are utilized at an identical or similar frequency. At moderate range of perceived stress, problem-focused coping appears to be more prevalent. At high levels of stress, emotion-focused coping appears to predominate.

Lazarus and Folkman further contended that some situations offer few opportunities to utilize problem-focused coping strategies, which may limit the utilization of that technique for adaptation. Limited options to manipulate the environment and utilize problem-focused coping are considerations with females who experienced massive traumatization during internment in the Auschwitz Concentration Camp setting.

However, emotion-focused coping strategies are "by no means passive, but have to do with internal restructuring" (Lazarus 1991). People typically utilize emotion-focused coping when they determine that avoidance of reality is more appropriate than direct confrontation. In such situations, individuals usually compare emotion-focused strategies, such as distancing, numbing, avoidance and denial, with problem-focused strategies, such as acts of resistance, task-oriented skills and manipulation of the external environment, when deciding how to maximize the negative consequences of massive traumatization.

Generally, people utilize problem-focused coping when an appraisal indicates that something concrete can be accomplished, where it may produce a positive change. People utilize emotion-focused coping when an appraisal indicates that nothing can be accomplished and to contend with loss and events that will not change loss, such as death.

Positive outcomes are associated with some coping strategies and negative outcomes with others. Some coping strategies are more stable than others. In addition, coping patterns differ with differing stressful encounters and differing individuals. Men and women use similar coping patterns despite beliefs that they do not.

Lazarus and Folkman (1984) concluded that coping includes all means to manage a stressful situation and that no one strategy can be considered inherently better than another. The appropriateness of a specific strategy is dependent upon a given circumstance, which is determined only by the strategy's effects in the long term.

Lazarus and Folkman also contended that people use denial or denial-like processes when nothing constructive can be done to overcome threat or harm, major illness or loss of a loved one. Salamon (1994) suggested a theory indicating that denial and avoidance typically have been categorized as defense mechanisms commonly used by Holocaust victims. He stated that concentration-camp survivors suffering daily torture and massive traumatization utilized the defense mechanisms of denial, repression and negation.

HOLOCAUST COPING STRATEGIES

Dimsdale (1974, 1978, 1980) explored coping strategies in his investigations of Holocaust survivors. He theorized that survivors' coping strategies include twelve classifications, including the following:

1. Focus on the good (looking for small gratification)
2. Survival for some purpose (to bear witness, seek revenge, help others)

3. Humor (insulation from reality and mediator of stress)
4. Psychological removal (insulating self from others, Musulman or walking death)
5. Time focusing (thinking of another time or place)
6. Mastery of the environment (maintaining some form of dignity or mastery internally or externally)
7. The will to live (discovery of a purpose or desire not to surrender to adversity)
8. Hope (active hope which is a conviction that an end is near, or passive that where there is life, there is hope)
9. Group affiliation (friendships and assistance for and from others)
10. Regressive behaviors (crying, acting as a child, vulnerability)
11. Fatalism (null coping or relying on others or fate)
12. Surrendering to stress (an anti-coping to stress)

Bruno Bettelheim (1960), one of the first psychologists to study the effects of coping on concentration-camp survivors, suggested that coping involves intellectual withdrawal, identification with the aggressor or a Musulman effect.

Des Pres (1976), Dimsdale (1980) and Frankl (1984, 1988) suggested that survivors coped by using the will to live and finding a meaning or purpose to survive. Des Pres also concluded that survivors used a splitting technique to separate themselves from their environments while observing what was occurring. Coping, in his opinion, also involved stealing, acts of resistance, suicide, smuggling and focusing on day-to-day tasks.

Viktor Frankl (1984, 1988), a noted psychotherapist and Holocaust survivor, contended that an existential technique, which utilized the discovery of a meaning in life, motivated people to be strong enough to survive. According to Frankl

(1984), "The striving to find a meaning in one's life is the primary motivational force in man." Frankl believed the uniqueness of each person's meaning to be as individual as each person. Even a tragic or unavoidable circumstance may be turned into a personal learning experience and may produce human achievement through the meaning of the lesson. The challenge lies in humans discovering meaning and importance for themselves. Frankl contended that survivors' acquisition of meaning occurred through three distinct pathways: creating or accomplishing a deed or goal; experiencing goodness, affiliation with others, truth or beauty; and discovering meaning in the midst of unavoidable suffering.

POST-TRAUMATIC STRESS DISORDER (PTSD)

Psychological disorders related to combat stress were first discussed after the American Civil War and termed "soldier's heart," describing a strain due to the stress of war (cited in Kleber and Brom 1992). Freud introduced the term "shell shock" during World War I when he used the German term Kriegsneurosen or "war neuroses." Criteria in the *Diagnostic and Statistical Manual (DSM-I)* defined shell shock as gross stress reaction with war or acute traumatic neurosis.

Research on the veterans of the Korean and Vietnam Wars has connected stress and combat experience. With increasing awareness of the psychosocial impairments related to stress reactions during World War II and the Vietnam War, the syndrome known as post-traumatic stress disorder (PTSD) has received substantial attention. Kleber and Brom (1992) stated that 15.2 percent of all male Vietnam veterans and 8.5 percent of all female Vietnam veterans met the criteria for PTSD, with an additional

11.1 percent of male and 7.8 percent of female Vietnam veterans suffering from other clinical stress reactions (836,000 veterans of the United States with full or partial stress disorders).

The PTSD patient is defined with the following criteria: The person experienced, witnessed or was confronted with events that involved threatened death or serious injury to themselves or others; the response involved horror, helplessness or intense fear; the individual persistently reexperiences the traumatic event; the person avoids the stimulus and experiences numbing; the person experiences increased arousal *(Diagnostic and Statistical Manual for Mental Disorders [DSM-IV])*. The *DSM-IV* describes the symptomatology of persons unable to cope as inability to discontinue thoughts, images, or perceptions related to the trauma, recurring frightening dreams, hallucinations, hypervigilance, irritability or outbursts of anger, flashbacks, detachments, and avoidance of people, places, or activities. Symptomatology and effects of PTSD resulting from massive traumatization have been reported by survivors of the Holocaust, POWs, veterans of the Vietnam War (Parson 1988) and Cambodian refugees (Kinzie 1988). Hunter (1988) suggested it is essential "to look at those common psychological residuals of captivity, regardless of war or time in history, that persist to impact the psychosocial adjustment of former captives."

MASSIVE TRAUMATIZATION

Parson (1988) believed that those who have endured extreme stress or massive traumatization suffer a "profound rupture in the very fabric of the self." Des Pres (1976), Dimsdale (1980), Kahana et al. (1988), Krystal (1968), Lifton (1980, 1986), Spiegelman (1986, 1991) and Wiesel (1985) agree that the traumatization experienced due to extreme stress ruptures the survivor's world deep into its very core.

Kahana et al. (1988) said that extreme stress or traumatization has six aspects:

1. Total life is disrupted and the fabric of normal life has become disconnected from reality.
2. The new situation is hostile, threatening, horrific and dangerous.
3. The ability to create change and remove the stressors is limited.
4. There appears to be no predictable end to the extreme stress or traumatization.
5. There is pain, suffering, and life appears meaningless and irrational, with no anchoring or means of predicting what might occur.
6. Moral principles—good and bad, evil and right—seem to have no place within this setting.

Cohen (1953) and Kahana et al. (1988) determined that prisoners living under extreme stress or massive traumatization experience little choice of outcomes and are relatively helpless. A high predominance of chance exists in their situations, compared to situations with ordinary stressors in which individuals can use a variety of coping strategies. However, Cordell (1982) suggested that those exposed to extreme massive traumatization are confronted with having absolutely no certainty, and certainty is necessary for adequate coping strategies.

Benner, Roskies and Lazarus (1980) contended that concentration-camp experiences differ from other massive traumatizations because of three elements. First, a persistent and consistent threat from a hostile force was present, with no place for escape. It is apparent that concentration camps were systematically organized to destroy the soul and fiber of the prisoners by stripping them of their support and personal identities. Second, the ability of the survivors to affect the environment was severely limited. Coping by use of problem solving, such as deciding to eat now or eat later, could only affect small segments of life. Third, the opportunity was limited for a prisoner to discover a means of coping by finding meaning or purpose in the genocide and atrocities. The Jewish people had known suffering in their collective past, but the "suffering inflicted by the Holocaust had no ultimate good, reward or meaning inherent in it."

Kleber and Brom (1992) suggested that the extreme long-lasting effects of massive traumatization on concentration-camp survivors can only be understood after examination of the events during captivity. They contended that the extreme conditions included prisoner humiliation; crude violence; verbal, sexual and physical abuse; separation from loved ones; constant threat of death to self and others; horrific living conditions; negligent hygienic conditions; hunger and absolute hopelessness. Chodoff (1970) reported that a psychological survival depended on his or her ability to cope with daily humiliation and abuse at the hands of the Nazis. Self-preservation behavior became a necessity in the disruption of reality.

Cohen (1953), Des Pres (1976) and Frankl (1984, 1988) spoke about the central themes of prisoners' thoughts. Bettelheim spoke of survivors returning to primitive emotional stages of development during massive traumatization. Frankl (1984) reported that prisoners of concentration camps experienced phases of massive traumatization that included shock (a numbing or shut-down mechanism) and apathy (an emotional death in which reality dims and emotions surround self-preservation). Chodoff (1986) agreed that concentration-camp inmates experienced shock, followed by apathy and, thereafter, more active coping mechanisms for self-preservation.

SEARCH FOR MEANING

Viktor Frankl identified the coping strategy of finding meaning or purpose within suffering. Although no purpose can be identified for the actual suffering, victims gained strength through identifying their own individual purposes for existence (Benner, Roskies and Lazarus 1980). In Frankl's *Man's Search for Meaning* (1984), he shared his philosophy of this coping strategy, which contended that meaning in life includes suffering and death. Finding a meaning or purpose for living included the courage to maintain hope that life could be reconstructed by those who remained strong. Frankl stated, "It is possible to practice the art of living even in a concentration camp, although suffering is omnipresent." The Nazis could take everything from a prisoner, but they could not take away one's choice of attitude in any situation. One chose whether or not to submit to those who threatened to rob one's very soul.

Des Pres (1976) believed that fear and beatings drove concentration-camp prisoners. He contended that all organisms strive to find protection within their environments and seek coping strategies. Prisoners knew they had the choice of committing to live through a day or giving up. Des Pres agreed with Frankl that prisoners went through phases of survival, but he suggested that the first stage, which is similar to Frankl's, is that of "initial collapse." The breakdown is followed by a stage of reintegration and recovery to a stable selfhood. He believed that prisoners survived and moved from withdrawal to self-preservation and forms of resistance.

Bettelheim (1960) stated that if the desire to live is lost, if a prisoner does not move through the initial collapse, the prisoner will lose his or her inner strength and will soon die. Survivors realized that life must go on, if only through routine and habit. Krystal (1968) and Lifton (1986) suggested that this initial stage is generally short-term in duration and that coping strategies generally include dissociation, denial, shock or disbelief. Benner, Roskies and Lazarus (1980) noted that selective apathy and denial were essential for life. Eitinger (1983) believed that the second stage is met with coping strategies, emotional numbing or some choices while confronting the environment.

Des Pres (1976) noted that survivors did not choose their imprisoned destiny and would find a means of escape if they could discover one. They were trapped in a world filled with Nazi domination, where dehumanization and total annihilation of Jewish people were proclaimed by the powers who held control. "The concentration camps were *in* this world and yet *not in* this world, places where behavior was grossly exaggerated, without apparent logic, yet fiercely hostile and encompassing." Those who experienced extreme massive traumatization have been changed forever. The success of coping strategies of survivors is that they were able "to come through; to keep a living soul in a living body."

APPENDIX C: WOMEN IN
DOUBLE JEOPARDY

Appendix C explores the unique vulnerability of women who were in "double jeopardy" during the Holocaust. Women's voices—different in many cases from men's voices—have often been ignored by male theorists, researchers, historians and fellow survivors.

Consequently, I offer a new "voice," one of interpretation, one that speaks of the adaptation and resiliency of women during massive traumatization. Gender-specific coping strategies that have often been ignored within Holocaust literature are reviewed and examined within this appendix, with full bibliographical citations provided in the references.

WOMEN'S UNIQUE VULNERABILITY

The atrocities of genocide were implemented with interconnected methods to choke the life from all facets of Jewish existence. This intentional "Final Solution" was only made possible by targeting Jewish women specifically as women, for they were the childbearers, the only ones able to ensure the continuity of Jewish life (Heinemann 1986; Ringelheim 1993; Rittner and Roth 1993). Ringelheim, as well as Rittner and Roth, presented sound evidence that the survival rate was much lower for Jewish women than for Jewish men. Jewish men may have perished at a quicker rate than females until 1942, but statistics illustrate that the overall loss of life during the Shoah was greater for Jewish women.

Gender was clearly not a neutral issue for the Nazis. Jewish women were the link to the destiny of the Jewish nation, and their annihilation was necessary for the completion of Hitler's plan for the creation of a superior Aryan nation. Joan Ringelheim, the Director of Oral History at the United States Holocaust Memorial Museum, wrote (1993), "Jewish women were to be killed not simply as Jewish women who may carry and give birth to the next generation of Jews. Although all Jews were to be killed, Jewish women's death and survival rate were dependent upon two obvious descriptions: Jewishness and femaleness."

When the figures are considered, it is easy to see why women had less of a chance to survive than men. There were two hundred women and one thousand men on Schindler's list. Ten women and three hundred men inhabited Debica, another labor camp. None of these numbers can make us sanguine about the possibilities for either Jewish women or Jewish men to survive, but they add to the growing impression that Nazi policy allowed for the possibility of more Jewish men than Jewish women to survive and that the Jewish councils, either through ignorance or acknowledgment of the situation, decided to save Jews—which often meant the saving of Jewish men (Ringelheim 1993).

The voices of the Holocaust predominantly have been those of men. The experiences, historical depiction and analysis have come principally from a male perspective. The classic works of our time celebrate the masterpieces of men, who have interwoven various disciplines, and include writers, psychologists, theologians, philosophers, historians, scholars and those who speak with their own voices as survivors. Men such as Yehuda Bauer (1982, 1989), Bruno Bettelheim (1960), Terrence Des Pres (1976), Joel Dimsdale (1974, 1978, 1980), Viktor Frankl (1984, 1988), Martin Gilbert (1981, 1985), Raul Hilberg (1985), Primo Levi (1965, 1993), Art Spiegelman (1986, 1991) and Elie Wiesel (1985) have led the way in Holocaust studies for generations. Their research added to our understanding of survivors at large. In shaping our understanding, these monumental works have influenced our insight, perceptions and interpretations of a systematic genocidal annihilation that is incomprehensible from a "human" perspective.

Women, however, were in double jeopardy. Gender became an issue when the Nazis realized they could accomplish annihilation of the species only by sterilizing or exterminating women. Women and men faced sexual and physical abuse. However, women were subject to atrocities that men rarely experienced or reported. They were raped and forced to have abortions, they were forced into prostitution, and the Nazis made women kill their own babies, as well as other children. Some pregnant women were thrown alive into the crematoria. Those with children were generally chosen in death selections. Many were separated from their young, while others were forced to make the "choiceless choice" of selecting one child instead of another in an effort to save at least one child from impending death. To overlook such intricate feminine issues is to negate women's unique experiences. The thoughts, feelings and perspectives of women in Auschwitz reveal distinctions unique only to females. By understanding gender-influenced differences in coping mechanisms and adaptations, we can better understand the research findings about gender-related defense mechanisms and survival strategies.

Heinemann (1986) emphasized gender-specific differences,

noting "to assume that Holocaust literature by men represents the writings of women is to remain blind to the findings of scholarship about the significance of gender in history and literature. Men and women live in different cultural spheres in all societies and have experienced many historical epochs and turning points in quite different ways. Until examination has shown whether men and women experienced and wrote about the Holocaust in the same way, research that implies the 'universality' of men's writing and experiences will be inadequate."

GENDER-SPECIFIC COPING MECHANISMS

The Nazi ideology encouraged the fertility of German women while exterminating pregnant Jewish women. This dichotomy created a society in which women living outside concentration camps were punished for their infertility, while mothers and children living within concentration-camp walls were murdered for their fertility. The Nazis believed that Jewish women had to be eliminated to ensure that the "vermin" that "infected" the Aryan nation would be destroyed.

For centuries, the unique experiences and coping strategies of women were ignored. The voice of the survivor was encapsulated into one voice, predominantly male. Women's specific means of coping and adapting to the genocidal atrocities of the Holocaust were silenced by males who generalized the "meaning" of all who bore witness. However, survivors, researchers and historians such as Charlotte Delbo (1992, 1993), Marlene Heinemann (1986), Isabella Leitner (1985, 1994), Joan Ringelheim (1984, 1985, 1993), Carol Rittner and John Roth (1993), Nechama Tec (1986) and Bonnie Gurewitsch (1998) have discussed the Shoah from a different perspective, focusing on the feelings, coping strategies and traumas that express the "invisible female voice."

Psychologist Carol Gilligan (1993) contended that the unique reflections of women have, for too long, been silenced by the male perspective, which has generalized men's thoughts and concepts as universal to all human systems.

In Rittner and Roth (1993), Ringelheim stated that Fagin and Ozick have been severely criticized for their gender-related conclusions. Rittner and Roth noted the view that gender-specific focusing contains the potential to denigrate the Holocaust, reducing it to sexism and detracting from the experiences of the survivors. They also noted the view that the genocide and atrocities perpetrated by the Third Reich were against Jews as Jews, not against men, women or children.

Viktor Frankl (1984, 1988), one of the most noted Holocaust survivors, believed that survivors identified with a "meaning or will to survive" as a means of coping with the traumatization of the Holocaust. Rappaport's work (1991) on the coping strategies and methods of adaptation incorporated by massive traumatization survivors during the Holocaust suggested the use of different forms of gender-specific coping techniques in the development of "meaning" for survival. That research revealed that women tended to cope by bonding emotionally to others, while men utilized coping mechanisms such as task orientation. Belle (cited in Monat and Lazarus 1991) agreed that women value and define themselves in terms of their relationships. In addition, women have been perceived as intensive, versus extensive, in terms of their relationships.

Rosenbaum (1993) reported that group affiliation was necessary for women's physical and emotional survival. Traditional male roles defined men as protectors and task-oriented, while traditional female roles defined women as nurturers, caregivers and creators of bonding with others. Rosenbaum contended that women were able to achieve their traditional role identities more easily than their male counterparts. For instance, in Auschwitz males used problem-focused strategies to cope. Frankl observed that males survived because they had created a "meaning or purpose" for their daily existence.

Concurring with the findings of Ringelheim (1984, 1985, 1993) and Heineman (1986), these hypotheses appear consistent with the gender-related studies of Gilligan (1993). Current theorists and researchers John Gray (1993) and Deborah Tannen (1990) suggested that female gender-oriented search for "meaning" is commonly directed toward relationships with others.

Seeking Help

Belle (1991) noted that women seek out support more readily than do men during times of stress. Belle remarked that females typically seek help and assistance when faced with problems and need for emotional support. For instance, Guta W. (see chapter 10) beseeched not only a German woman guard for help to save her mother but Eichmann himself. She knew no fear when it came to helping save her mother. Women also have shown a propensity to seek out more formal and informal sources of support and affiliation during stress than do males.

Belle also suggested that gender-specific differences relate to the loss of loved ones and that women appear less vulnerable than male counterparts due to the use of support networks. Anna Pawelcznśka (1979) contended that every female survivor of Auschwitz found support and encouragement from her fellow prisoners. Women assisted other women and thus helped maintain female emotional strength and resiliency when facing the dehumanizing acts of the Nazi regime.

Moral Decisions

Sociologist Carol Gilligan observed that women make moral judgments by relating to the conflicts and choices of their male counterparts. Her research illustrated that females made choices on the basis of their responsibility to nurture others within their circle of focus. Moral decisions involve concern for affiliation, caring for others' needs, alleviating hurt and pain for others and caring for others' feelings. "Care becomes the self-chosen principle of a judgment that remains psychological in its concern with relationships and response but becomes universal in its condemnation of exploitation and hurt" (Gilligan 1993).

Dr. Gisella Perl (1993), a survivor of Auschwitz, was "selected" by Dr. Josef Mengele to run a hospital ward within the death camp. Perl was forced to make "choiceless choices," such as whether to save the lives of pregnant mothers or to save their babies. Forced to make such no-win decisions, Perl chose to save mothers at the expense of killing their babies. Perl stated, "I had to remain alive . . . it was up to me to save the life of the mother, if there was no other way than by destroying the life of the unborn baby." Dramatically illustrated, this dilemma became a moral decision that ultimately defined Dr. Perl's meaning for survival. With no medicines, bandages, drugs or instruments, the only means of assisting others was through words of encouragement, comfort, nurturing and kindness.

Other researchers have confirmed Gilligan's approach to women's moral decisions. Clearly, women's decisions are based on meaning, which includes a dimension of concern and caring for others whom they value. In their masterpiece, *Different Voices: Women and the Holocaust,* Rittner and Roth (1993) concurred with Frankl and Gilligan and presented a compilation of female survivors' narratives that bear witness to personal interpretations of "meaning" and moral choices. Their work makes it clear that establishing binding relationships was a critical factor for many survivors. Rosenbaum (1993) contended, "Those seeking survival had to rebuild themselves through rebuilding their communal ties and vice versa." Reestablishing a new community or family by bonding with other women assisted the surviving prisoners in creating a reason to live.

Nurturing Relationships

Establishing and nurturing relationships appear to be powerful elements in a woman's search for meaning. In Ringelheim's (1993) research with survivors, she reported that all of her subjects spoke of having relationships with other women for support and encouragement. A survivor named Rose told Ringelheim, "Women's friendship is different than men's friendship, you see. . . . We have these motherly instincts, friend instincts more. . . . But that's what was holding the women together because everybody had to have someone to lean on, to depend on. The men, no . . . the men didn't do that."

Another survivor quoted in Ringelheim's work declared, "These women supported me physically . . . emotionally and spiritually. . . . Without this protection, I would have died. . . . Always part of some group of women for whom you went through fire. . . . You knew your group cared for you. . . . It was the reciprocity that kept you alive and going."

In contrast, Holocaust literature rarely explores the importance of friendships or relationships in men's personal narratives.

Maintaining Dignity

For many others, maintaining dignity was the force that contained meaning for survival. Survivors motivated themselves to maintain personal dignity by declaring that they had made the moral and conscious choice to die if they were selected. Abandoning that struggle meant giving in to the desires and wishes of the Nazis and their ideology. Losing one's dignity meant losing and becoming like the many Muselmänner, condemned to self-inflicted mental death and facing the end of perceived physical and psychological resources.

It was quite obvious that the Nazi concentration-camp procedure was designed to ultimately destroy the self-esteem and dignity of each of its prisoners. Isabella Leitner (1994) concurred with the meaning derived from the attempt to maintain dignity. She wrote in her memoir, "My body is nearly dead, but my vision is throbbing with life—even here. I want you to live for the very life that is yours."

Prisoners lost their identities, their names, their families, their personal possessions, their food, their ability to maintain bodily functions and even their hair. *Twenty Months at Auschwitz,* a poignant narrative by Pelagia Lewinska (1968), portrayed the strength of the human spirit. One means of defying the Nazis was to maintain even the smallest amount of dignity in personal care. For some, it was protecting their clothing from disease-infested lice; for others maintenance of cleanliness to the best of their ability; many resisted personal soiling; but for Lewinska, it was the cleaning of her boots each night. She reported, "It was our part in an act of protest which said: We will not let ourselves be broken!" (Rittner and Roth 1993). Focusing on appearance was a way of maintaining a part of one's prewar identity.

Maintaining physical appearances could be the deciding factor in the life or death of a woman threatened by Mengele's selection. The Nazis believed that a woman's physical appearance determined her bodily strength and, ultimately, her fate.

Resistance and Bearing Witness

Some women derived meaning from the belief that they must stay alive in order to bear witness for those who could not speak. The voices that exited from the chimneys could only be heard through those who lived to speak the truth. Auschwitz resistance fighters Anna Heilmann and Rose Meth (1993) found motivation for survival in their promise to bear witness to famous resistance fighters, such as Gisi Fleischman (who helped run an underground railroad to get Jews out of Poland) and Haika Grossman (a resistance fighter in Bialystok) and Marla Zimetbaum (the first woman to escape from Auschwitz, whose suicidal defiance at the gallows was a legendary act of resistance that motivated others to discover a meaning for life and death).

Heilmann and Meth chose to aid a resistance movement in 1944 that smuggled gunpowder from the factory to the Sonderkommando to destroy Crematorium IV in the Auschwitz death camp. Their acts of resistance paid tribute to other resistance fighters who were hanged when caught by the SS. Those brave women inspired others to face unbelievable danger through resistance. Their narratives include this statement (Heilmann and Meth 1993): "We were all going to die, but were not giving our lives for nothing. . . . We, too, decided that we were not going to let ourselves be taken without a struggle." Prisoners' resistance also took the form of denial of the Nazi goal to dehumanize and annihilate the human spirit. During each moment that a woman resisted the dehumanization, her noncompliance constituted an active show of resistance.

Using Humor

Lipman (1991) suggested that many survivors believe humor played a vital role in their coping and adaptation. Humor contained the light of hope used as a psychological weapon and a bond among trusted friends. Humor became a diversion, a shield and a lighthearted morale booster for those struggling with adversity. Humor became a form of personal resistance, a means of detaching from reality and a way to depersonalize the atrocities that were part of lives tortured daily: "In short, a cryptic redefining of the victim's world."

Luck

Livia Jackson (1993) believed that nearly all Auschwitz victims knew their survival had something to do with an element of luck. Many believe that luck had more to do with their survival than anything under their own control. "The choices people made—'choiceless' or not—did make a difference, but factors such as the following probably mattered just as much, if not more: a person's age and sex; when one was deported; whether he or she could ward off sickness; whether one might draw a work assignment that would reduce energy output or enable one to obtain better food; whether one could avoid the punishing whims of guards or the caprice of periodic selections; whether there was help of any kind that one could count on."

It was a common hypothesis, however, that survival was luck, but "true living" (Frankl's "will for meaning") occurred because survivors discovered a meaning in their continued forge onward despite the atrocities around them.

Frankl's (1984) approach revealed that despite such tremendous human-induced atrocities and unending suffering, a victim in extreme circumstances, within which no hope appears to exist, can exceed the limits of what seems possible. Frankl stated, "He (she) may turn a personal tragedy into a triumph."

Despite the monstrous number of females murdered, surviving Jewish women continue to bear witness and celebrate their ability to survive. Through oral histories, narratives and autobiographies, their personal stories celebrate the "meaning" that kept them ever-striving to survive despite seemingly insurmountable odds. Whether due to luck, technical skills, non-Jewish appearance, hope of reunion, faith, humor, personal resistance, or with the assistance of, or through, a relationship with another, these women survived, holding on valiantly to the "will to live!"

GLOSSARY

Aktion: A roundup of Jews.

Appell: Roll call of prisoners in the camps.

Aryan: As used by the Nazis, a (supposed) master race of non-Jewish Caucasians with Nordic features.

block: Prisoner housing, barrack.

Blockälteste: Prisoner appointed by the SS to be responsible for the blocks.

death march: Forced march of concentration-camp inmates near the end of the war when Germany was collapsing.

deportation: Transportation or resettlement of Jews to concentration camps or work camps.

Einsatzgruppen: SS mobile killing unit.

emotion-focused coping: Coping that utilizes "thinking" strategies.

Final Solution: Extermination of the Jews, specifically as proposed by Adolf Hitler.

Gestapo: An abbreviation for the Secret State Police of Nazi Germany (Geheime Stadtspolizei).

Jew: As defined by the Third Reich, a person descended from two Jewish grandparents or a person married to a Jew on or before September 15, 1935 (also see Mischlinge).

Jude, Juden: A name for Jews.

Judenrein: A cleansing or clearing of Jews from a locale.

Kanada: The depot for personal effects stolen from prisoners.

Kapo: Prisoner appointed to be in charge of the labor force.

Kristallnacht: "The Night of the Broken Glass," referring to November 9 and 10, 1938, when Nazis burned Jewish synagogues, homes and businesses.

Lager: A camp.

Lagerältester: The highest rank that could be obtained by a prisoner, a "camp elder."

Lagerführer: The head of a concentration camp section.

Lauferin: A gofer for anyone needing assistance.

Mischlinge: Nazi term for someone part Jewish under Nuremberg racial laws.

Musulman: A person facing the end of his or her physical and psychological resources; a "living corpse" or "living dead."

pogrom: A violent attack on Jews by non-Jews including rape, murder and looting of property.

POW: Prisoner of war.

problem-focused coping: Coping that is action-centered in nature.

Selektion: Selection of who would live to work as slave labor and who would die.

Shoah: Hebrew term for Holocaust, meaning "catastrophe" or "fire."

Sonderkommando: Jewish prisoners forced by the Nazis to work in the gas chambers and crematoria.

SS: Schutzstaffel, elite Nazi guards under Heinrich Himmler.

Stubendienst: A helper.

taleisim, tallis, tallit: Prayer shawls.

untermenschen: Subhumans.

Zyklon B: Poisonous cyanide gas used for mass extermination in the gas chambers.

CHRONOLOGY OF EVENTS

1933

January 30	Hitler becomes chancellor of Germany. Jews feel effects of anti-Jewish polices.
March 20	The first concentration camp at Dachau is established.

1935

September 15	Nuremberg Laws are established, which contain Reich Citizenship Law, stating that German citizens are those with "German or related blood," and the Law for the Protection of German Blood and Honor, which prohibits marriage or sexual relations between German non-Jews and Jews.
November 15	First Ordinance to Reich Citizenship specifies that a Jew cannot be a Reich citizen.

1938

June 15	1,500 German Jews are sent to concentration camps.
October 5	The passports of German Jews are marked with a "J" for Jude.

November 9–10   "Night of the Broken Glass," or Kristallnacht,
                destroys Jewish synagogues and businesses;
                30,000 Jews interned in camps.
November 15   Jewish children excluded from German
                schools.

1939

January 30   Hitler declares that world war will mean the
                "annihilation of the Jewish race in Europe."
May 15   Ravensbruck, the first women's camp, is
                established.
May 18   The first women arrive at Ravensbruck.
June 29   Austrian Gypsy females are deported to
                Ravensbruck.
September 1   Germany invades Poland.
September 3   Great Britain and France declare war on
                Germany.
September 9   World War II begins.
September 17   Russian troops invade Poland and occupy half
                of the country.
September 28   Germany and Russia divide Poland.
November 23   Jews in occupied Poland are forced to wear a
                Jewish Star of David.

1940

January   First experimental gassing of Jews and other
                "undesirables" occurs.
February 8   Lodz ghetto is established.
April–June   Germany invades Norway, Holland, Denmark,
                France and Belgium.

April 27   Himmler orders the establishment of Auschwitz
                in Oswiecim, Poland.
April 30   Lodz ghetto is sealed.
November   Warsaw ghetto is established.

1941

March 1   Himmler travels to Auschwitz and orders addi-
                tional facilities and the construction of
                Birkenau (Auschwitz II). Prisoners are avail-
                able for forced labor to construct I. G. Farben.
March 3   Adolf Eichmann is appointed head of the
                Gestapo's Section for Jewish Affairs.
April   Germany invades Yugoslavia and Greece.
June 22   Germany invades Russia. Poland comes under
                total control of Germany.
July 31   Hermann Göring signs orders giving Reinhard
                Heydrich authority to prepare the "Final
                Solution of the Jewish question."
September 3   The first experiment with Zyklon B takes place
                in Auschwitz.
September 29–30 The Einsatzkommando murders 33,000 Jews
                in Babi Yar, near Kiev.
October 15   From Czechoslovakia, Germany, Austria and
                Luxembourg, 20,000 Jews are deported east-
                ward to ghettos.
October   The Theresienstadt ghetto and concentration
                camp is established.
December 7   Japan attacks Pearl Harbor. United States
                declares war on Japan.
December 11   United States declares war on Germany.

1942

January 20	Wannsee Conference establishes doctrine for the "Final Solution."
February 15	First people are killed with Zyklon B in Auschwitz.
March 1	First inmates moved to Birkenau (Auschwitz II).
March 20	Farmhouse renovated as gas chambers in Auschwitz-Birkenau.
March 26	Separate women's camp established in Auschwitz. First Slovak Jews sent to Auschwitz.
March 27	First French Jews deported to Auschwitz.
May 4	The first "selection" takes place for those who have been imprisoned in Auschwitz for months. The unfit are sent to gas chambers.
July 4	First selection at the railroad unloading platforms in Auschwitz takes place.
July 7	Heinrich Himmler agrees to experimentation with Jewish women in Auschwitz.
July 15	Jews are deported from Westerbork. Anne Frank and her family are deported to Auschwitz.
July 19	Heinrich Himmler orders complete extermination of Polish Jews by the end of the year.
July–September	Approximately 300,000 Jews are deported en masse from the Warsaw ghetto.
August 1	Deportation of Jews from Belgium.
December	Gypsies deported to Auschwitz.

1943

January 18	First Warsaw ghetto uprising breaks out.
March–June	Four gas chambers and crematoria are operational in Auschwitz-Birkenau.
April 19–May 16	Additional Warsaw ghetto uprising and final destruction of ghetto.
Mid-June	Heinrich Himmler orders liquidation of all remaining ghettos.
July 11	Hitler bans public reference to the "Final Solution of the Jewish question."
October 1–2	Danes rescue 7,200 Danish Jews.
December	First transport of Austrian Jews to Auschwitz takes place.

1944

March 19	Germany occupies Hungary.
April 9	Two Jews escape from Auschwitz, and news of terrors spread.
April	Jews are mandated to wear the Star of David.
May 15	First transport of Hungarian Jews to Auschwitz takes place.
June 6	D-Day: Allied forces land in Normandy.
August 2	A Gypsy family camp in Auschwitz is liquidated (2,897 prisoners).
October 7	A Sonderkommando revolt takes place in Auschwitz-Birkenau. Jewish women smuggle explosives and destroy Crematorium IV.
November	Killing with Zyklon B in gas chambers is discontinued.
November 26	Heinrich Himmler orders destruction of the crematoria in Auschwitz-Birkenau.

1945

January 6	Four female Jewish resistance fighters who smuggled explosives to Sonderkommando are hung.
January 17–18	Evacuation and forced march from Auschwitz-Birkenau takes place. Of 31,894 prisoners in the last roll call, 16,577 are reported to be female.
April 11	U.S. forces liberate Buchenwald.
April 15	British forces liberate Bergen-Belsen.
April 29–30	Russian forces liberate Ravensbruck.
April 30	Hitler and Eva Braun commit suicide.
May 7	V-E Day: Germany surrenders.
November 17	Nuremberg war-crime trials begin. Twenty women, including Irma Grese, are sentenced to death.

REFERENCES

American Psychiatric Association. *Diagnostic and Statistical Manual of Mental Disorders DSM-IV.* 2d ed. Washington, D.C.: APA, 1994.

Bauer, Y. *A History of the Holocaust.* New York: Franklin Watts, 1982.

———. *Remembering for the Future: Working Papers and Addenda.* Vols. 1, 2, 3. Oxford, England: Pergamon Press, 1989.

Belle, D. "Gender Differences in the Social Moderators of Stress." In *Stress and Coping: An Anthology.* Edited by A. Monat and R. S. Lazarus. New York: Columbia University Press, 1991.

Benner, P., E. Roskies, and R. S. Lazarus. "Stress and Coping under Severe Conditions." In *Survivors, Victims, and Perpetrators.* Edited by J. E. Dimsdale. Washington, D.C.: Hemisphere, 1980.

Berenbaum, M. *The World Must Know: The History of the Holocaust as Told in the U.S. Holocaust Memorial Museum.* Boston: Little, Brown & Company, 1993.

Bettelheim, B. 1943. "Individual and Mass Behavior in Extreme Situations." *Journal of Abnormal and Social Psychology* 33, no. 4 (1943): 417–52.

———. *The Informed Heart.* New York: The Free Press, 1960.

Billings, A. G., and R. H. Moos. "The Role of Coping Responses and Social Resources in Attenuating the Stress of Life Events." *Journal of Behavioral Medicine* 4, no. 2 (1981).

Brill, N. Q., and B. W. Beebe. *A Follow-Up Study for War*

Neuroses. Washington, D.C.: Veterans Administration Medical Monograph, 1955.

Cannon, W. B. *The Wisdom of the Body.* New York: Norton, 1939.

Chodoff, P. "The German Concentration Camp as a Psychological Stress." *Archives of General Psychiatry* 22, no. 1 (1970): 78–87.

———. "Survivors of the Nazi Holocaust." *Children Today* 10 (September–October 1981): 2–5.

———. "Survivors of the Nazi Holocaust." In *Coping with Life Crisis: An Integrated Approach.* Edited by R. H. Moss. New York: Plenum Press, 1986.

Cofer, C. N., and M. H. Appley. *Motivation: Theory and Research.* New York: Wiley, 1964.

Cohen, E. A. *Human Behavior in the Concentration Camps.* New York: W. W. Norton, 1953.

Cordell, M. *Coping Behavior of Nazi Concentration Camp Survivors.* Doctoral Dissertation, Pacific Graduate School of Psychology, 1982.

Dawidowicz, L. *A Holocaust Reader.* West Orange, N.J.: Behrman House, Inc., 1976.

Delbo, C. *None of Us Will Return.* Translated by R. C. Lamont. New Haven: Yale University Press, 1992.

———. "Arrivals, Departures." In *Different Voices: Women and the Holocaust.* Edited by C. Rittner and J. Roth. New York: Paragon House, 1993.

———. "Days and Memory." In *Different Voices: Women and the Holocaust.* Edited by C. Rittner and J. Roth. New York: Paragon House, 1993.

———. "Lulu." In *Different Voices: Women and the Holocaust.* Edited by C. Rittner and J. Roth. New York: Paragon House, 1993.

Des Pres, T. *The Survivor: The Anatomy of Life in the Death*

Camp. Oxford, England: Oxford University Press, 1976.

Dimsdale, J. E. "The Coping Behavior of Nazi Concentration Camp Survivors." *American Journal of Psychiatry* 131 (1974): 792–97.

———. "Coping: Every Man's War." *American Journal of Psychotherapy* 32, no. 3 (1978): 402–413.

———. *Survivors, Victims, and Perpetrators: Essays on the Nazi Holocaust.* New York: Taylor and Francis, 1980.

Edelheit, A., and H. Edelheit. *History of the Holocaust.* Boulder: Westview Press, 1994.

Eibeshitz, A., and J. Eibeshitz. *Women in the Holocaust.* New York: Remember, 1993.

———. *Women in the Holocaust.* Vol. 2. New York: Remember, 1994.

Eitinger, L. "Studies on Concentration Camp Survivors: The Norwegian and Global Context." *Journal of Psychology and Judaism* 6, no. 1 (1983): 23–32.

Elder, G. H., and E. C. Clipp. "Combat Experiences, Comradeship, and Psychological Health." In *Human Adaptation to Extreme Stress: From the Holocaust to Vietnam.* Edited by J. P. Wilson, Z. Harel, and B. Kahana. New York: Plenum Press, 1988.

Ellman, M. *Thinking About Women.* New York: Harcourt, Brace, and World, 1968.

Epstein, H. "Heirs of the Holocaust." *New York Times Magazine* (June 1977): 74–77.

———. *Children of the Holocaust: Conversations with Sons and Daughters of Survivors.* New York: Penguin Books, 1988.

Frankl, V. *Man's Search for Meaning.* New York: Washington Square Press, 1984.

———. *The Will to Meaning: Foundations and Applications of*

Logotherapy. New York: First Meridian Printing, 1988.

Gilbert, M. *Auschwitz and the Allies.* New York: Henry Holt and Company, 1981.

———. *The Holocaust: A History of the Jews of Europe During the Second World War.* New York: Henry Holt and Company, 1985.

Gilligan, C. *In a Different Voice: Psychological Theory and Women's Development.* Cambridge: Harvard University Press, 1993.

Gray, J. *Men Are from Mars, Women Are from Venus.* New York: Harper Collins Press, 1993.

Grinker, R. R., and J. P. Spiegel. *Men Under Stress.* New York: McGraw Hill, 1945.

Gurewitsch, B. *Mothers, Sisters, Resisters: Oral Histories of Women Who Survived the Holocaust.* Tuscaloosa: The University of Alabama Press, 1998.

Gutman, Y., and M. Berenbaum. *Anatomy of the Auschwitz Death Camp.* Bloomington: Indiana University Press, 1994.

Hann, N. "The Assessment of Coping, Defenses, and Stress." In *Handbook of Stress: Theoretical and Clinical Aspects.* Edited by L. Goldberger and S. Breznitz. New York: Free Press, 1982.

Heilmann, A., and R. Meth. "Resistance." In *Different Voices: Women and the Holocaust.* Edited by C. Rittner and J. Roth. New York: Paragon House, 1993.

Heinemann, M. *Gender and Destiny: Women Writers and the Holocaust.* New York: Greenwood Press, 1986.

Hilberg, R. *The Destruction of the European Jews: Student Edition.* New York: Holmes & Meyer, 1985.

Hunter, E. J. "The Psychological Effects of Being a Prisoner of War." In *Human Adaptation to Extreme Stress: From the Holocaust to Vietnam.* Edited by J. Wilson, Z. Harel, and B. Kahana. New York: Plenum Press, 1988.

Jackson, L. "Coming of Age." In *Different Voices: Women and the Holocaust.* Edited by C. Rittner and J. Roth. New York: Paragon House, 1993.

Jacobson, A. M. "Ego Defense Mechanisms Manual." In *Ego Mechanisms of Defense: A Guide for Clinicians and Researchers.* Edited by G. E. Vaillant. Washington, D.C.: American Psychiatric Press, Inc., 1986.

Kahana, E., B. Kahana, Z. Harel, and T. Rosner. "Coping with Extreme Trauma." In *Human Adaptation to Extreme Stress: From the Holocaust to Vietnam.* Edited by J.P. Wilson, Z. Harel, and B. Kahana. New York: Plenum Press, 1988.

Katz, E., and J. M. Ringelheim. "Women Surviving: The Holocaust." In *Proceedings of the Conference.* Institute for Research in History, Stern College, New York, 1983.

Kinzie, J. D. "The Psychiatric Effects of Massive Trauma on Cambodian Refugees." In *Human Adaptation to Extreme Stress: From the Holocaust to Vietnam.* Edited by J. P. Wilson, Z. Harel, and B. Kahana. New York: Plenum Press, 1988.

Kleber, R. J., and D. Brom. *Coping with Trauma: Theory, Prevention, and Treatment.* Amsterdam/Lisse: Swets & Zeitlinger, 1992.

Klein, C. *Sentenced to Live.* New York: Holocaust Library, 1988.

Krystal, H. "Studies of Concentration Camp Survivors." In *Massive Psychic Trauma.* Edited by H. Krystal. New York: International Universities Press, 1968.

Lawliss, C. *. . . and God Cried: The Holocaust Remembered.* New York: JG Press, 1994.

Lazarus, R. S. *Psychological Stress and the Coping Process.* New York: McGraw-Hill, 1966.

———. *Emotion and Adaptation.* New York: Oxford University Press, 1991.

————. "From Psychological Stress to the Emotions: A History of Changing Outlooks." *Annual Review of Psychology* 44 (1993): 1–21.

Lazarus, R. S., and C. W. Erickson. "Effects of Failure Stress upon Skilled Performance." *Journal of Experimental Psychology* 43 (1952): 100–105.

Lazarus, R. S., and Folkman, S. *Stress, Appraisal, and Coping.* New York: Springer, 1984.

Lazarus, R. S., and Launier, R. "Stress-Related Transactions Between Person and the Environment." In *Perspectives in Interactional Psychology.* Edited by L. A. Pervin and M. Lewis. New York: Plenum Press, 1978.

————. "Fragments of Isabella." In *Different Voices: Women and the Holocaust.* Edited by J. Rittner and C. Roth. New York: Paragon House, 1993.

Leitner, I., and I. Leitner. *Saving the Fragments: From Auschwitz to New York.* New York: New American Library, 1985.

————. *Isabella: From Auschwitz to Freedom.* New York: Anchor Books, 1994.

Levi, P. *The Reawakening.* New York: Collier Books, 1965.

————. *Survival in Auschwitz.* New York: Collier Books, 1993.

Lewinska, P. *Twenty Months at Auschwitz.* New York: Lyle Stuart, 1968. Also in *Different Voices: Women and the Holocaust.* Edited by C. Rittner and J. Roth. New York: Paragon House, 1993.

Lifton, R. J. "The Concept of the Survivor." In *Survivors, Victims, and Perpetrators: Essays on the Nazi Holocaust.* Edited by J. E. Dimsdale. New York: Taylor & Francis, 1980.

————. "Reflections on Genocide." *Psycho-History Review* 14, no. 3 (1986): 39–54.

Lipman, S. *Laughter in Hell: The Use of Humor During the Holocaust.* Northvale, N.J.: Jason Aronson Inc., 1991.

Marmar, C. R., and M. J. Horwitz. "Diagnostic and Phase-Oriented Treatment of Post-Traumatic Stress Disorder." In *Human Adaptation to Extreme Stress: From Holocaust to Vietnam.* Edited by J. P. Wilson, Z. Harel, and B. Kahana. New York: Plenum Press, 1988.

McCrae, R. R. "Situational Determinants of Coping Responses: Loss, Threat, and Challenge." *Journal of Personality and Social Psychology* 46 (1984): 919–28.

Meissner, W. "Meissner's Glossary of Defenses." In *Ego Mechanisms of Defense: A Guide for Clinicians and Researchers.* Edited by G. E. Vaillant. Washington, D.C.: American Psychiatric Press, Inc., 1981.

Merriam, S. B. *Case Study Research in Education: A Qualitative Approach.* San Francisco: Jossey-Bass Publishers, 1988.

Miles, M. B., and A. M. Huberman. *Qualitative Data Analysis.* 2d ed. Thousand Oaks, Ca.: Sage Publications, 1994.

Monat, A., and R. S. Lazarus. *Stress and Coping: An Anthology.* 3d ed. New York: Columbia University Press, 1991.

Parson, E. R. "Post-Traumatic Stress Disorders (PTSD): Theoretical and Practical Considerations in Psychotherapy of Vietnam War Veterans." In *Human Adaptation to Extreme Stress: From the Holocaust to Vietnam.* Edited by J. P. Wilson, Z. Harel, and B. Kahana. New York: Plenum Press, 1988.

Patton, M. Q. *Qualitative Evaluation and Research Methods.* 2d ed. Newbury Park, Ca.: Sage Publications, 1990.

Pawelczyńska, A. *Values and Violence in Auschwitz: A Sociological Analysis.* Translated by Catherine S. Leach. Berkeley: Ca.: University of California Press, 1979.

Perl, G. "A Doctor in Auschwitz." In *Different Voices: Women and the Holocaust.* Edited by C. Rittner and J. Roth. New York: Paragon House, 1993.

Perry, J. C. "Perry's Defense Mechanism Rating Scale." In *Ego Mechanisms of Defense: A Guide for Clinicians and Researchers.* Edited by G. E. Vaillant, Washington, D. C.: American Psychiatric Press, Inc., 1990.

Rappaport, S. *Coping and Adaptation to Massive Psychic Trauma: Case Studies of Nazi Holocaust Survivors.* Dissertation Abstract, Union Graduate School. University Microfilms No. 9202325, 1991.

Ringelheim, J. "The Unethical and the Unspeakable: Women and the Holocaust." *Simon Wiesenthal Center Annual* 1 (1984): 69–70.

———. "Women and the Holocaust." *Signs: Journal of Women in Culture and Society* 10, no. 4 (1985): 741–61.

———. "Women and the Holocaust: A Reconsideration of Research." In *Different Voices: Women and the Holocaust.* Edited by C. Rittner and J. Roth. New York: Paragon House, 1993.

Rittner, C., and J. Roth. *Different Voices: Women and the Holocaust.* New York: Paragon House, 1993.

Rosenbaum, J. F. *Female Experiences During the Holocaust.* Master's Thesis, Boston College. U.M.I. Dissertation Services No. 1353166, 1993.

Salamon, M. J. "Denial and Acceptance: Coping and Defense Mechanisms." *Clinical Gerontologist* 14, no. 3 (1994): 17–25.

Schleunes, K. A. *The Twisted Road to Auschwitz: Nazi Policy Toward German Jews 1933-1939.* Urbana: University of Illinois Press, 1990.

Schmolling, P. "Human Reactions to the Nazi Concentration

Camps: A Summing Up." *Journal of Human Stress* 10 (1984): 108–120.

Selye, H. *The Stress of Life.* New York: McGraw-Hill, 1956.

———. *Stress Without Distress.* New York: The New American Library, 1974.

Spiegelman, A. *Maus I: A Survivor's Tale—My Father Bleeds History.* New York: Pantheon Books, 1986.

———. *Maus II: A Survivor's Tale—And Here My Troubles Began.* New York: Pantheon Books, 1991.

Swiebocka, T., ed. *Auschwitz: A History in Photographs.* Oswiecim and Bloomington: Indiana University Press, 1990, 1993.

Tannen, D. *You Don't Understand Me: Men and Women in Conversation.* New York: Ballantine Press, 1990.

Taylor, S. J., and R. Bogdan. *Introduction to Qualitative Research Methods: The Search for Meanings.* New York: John Wiley & Sons, 1984.

Tec, N. *When Light Pierced the Darkness: Christian Rescue of Jews in Nazi-Occupied Poland.* New York: Oxford University Press, 1986.

United States Holocaust Institute Archives. Record Group-50, Oral History. Washington, D.C.: United States Holocaust Memorial Museum.

Vaillant, G. E. *Adaptation to Life.* Boston: Little, Brown & Company, 1977.

———. *Ego Mechanisms of Defense: A Guide for Clinicians and Researchers.* Washington D.C.: American Psychiatric Press, Inc., 1992.

———. *The Wisdom of Ego.* Cambridge: Harvard University Press, 1993.

Wiesel, E. *Night Trilogy.* New York: The Noonday Press, 1985.

Wilson, J., Z. Harel, and B. Kahana. *Human Adaptation to Extreme Stress: From the Holocaust to Vietnam.* New York: Plenum Press, 1988.

Yahil, L. *The Holocaust: The Fate of European Jewry.* New York: Oxford University Press, 1990.

INDEX

ABOUT THE AUTHOR

Joy Erlichman Miller, Ph.D., is an internationally known licensed psychotherapist, certified master addictions counselor, professional trainer and author. In her work as a motivational speaker, she draws large audiences with her humor and enthusiasm while involving them actively in her workshops. Miller is the founder and director of Joy Miller & Associates in Peoria. She has been involved professionally in the mental-health field for twenty-five years and teaches part-time in the graduate program at Bradley University.

Dr. Miller, a leading authority on relationship issues, has participated in over 150 international conferences and has worked with over 10,000 participants in the past ten years. She is a frequent guest expert on national syndicated television and has appeared on the Sally Jessy Raphael, Oprah Winfrey, Jenny Jones, Montel Williams and Geraldo Rivera talk shows. Her written works have been featured in various national magazines and more than thirty U.S. newspapers. Dr. Miller hosted her own radio show for five years on a CBS affiliate radio station and currently presents a twice-weekly mental-health segment, entitled "Moment for the Mind," during the nightly news on the Peoria-area CBS television affiliate. She has been the station's mental-health consultant for seven years. She also writes a weekly mental-health column, entitled "Mind Matters," for the *Peoria Times-Observer.*

In 1996, Dr. Miller received the Harold Hodgkinson

Dissertation Award for "The Coping Strategies and Adaptation Mechanisms Utilized by Female Holocaust Survivors from the Auschwitz Concentration Camp." This annual award is bestowed upon the Walden University doctoral-program graduate whose dissertation excels for its academic excellence and potential for publication. Dr. Miller has also received the Harold Baer Award and the Outstanding Alumni Award from Bradley University, as well as the Peg Burke Award from the Mental Health Association of Illinois Valley.

Dr. Miller was an interviewer for Steven Spielberg's *Survivors of the Shoah* project. She has interviewed survivors from the Peoria area and is the chairperson of the Peoria Holocaust Survivors Project. Currently she chairs Peoria's Yom Hashoah services and the March of the Living, and is a member of the Interfaith Alliance, which works to fight bigotry, racism and prejudice.

In the early 1990s, Dr. Miller and an associate created a teen crisis line which is still in existence. The Teen Line serves as an arm of Peoria's Crisis Line, which services all of the Peoria Tri-County area.

Dr. Miller is the author of five books published by Health Communications and Simcha Press, including *Following the Yellow Brick Road: The Adult Child's Personal Journey Through Oz, My Holding You Up Is Holding Me Back: Over-Responsibility and Shame, Celebrations for Your Inner Child*, her most noted work, *Addictive Relationships: Reclaiming Your Boundaries*, which has sold over sixty-five thousand copies and has recently been published in Chinese, and *Love Carried Me Home: Women Surviving the Holocaust*. She also has coauthored a counselor-training book, "A Transformation Journey," which is pending publication.

Dr. Miller is contributing all proceeds from *Love Carried Me*

Home: Women Surviving Auschwitz to the United States Holocaust Memorial Museum in honor of the sixteen women profiled within its pages.

For more information, Dr. Miller can be contacted at Joy Miller and Associates, 7617 N. Villa Wood Lane, Peoria, Illinois 61614, (309) 693-8200. You can also visit her Web page at *www.joymiller.com.*

New Releases from Simcha Press

Converting to Judaism
By Rabbi Bernice Kimel Weiss

Amazing, powerful, soul-stirring stories of re-creation—the extraordinary adventure of becoming a Jew at the turn of the 21st century.

Code #8202 • Quality Paperback • $9.95

Esther—A Jerusalem Love Story
By Dvora Waysman

A love story that is both magic and tragic! Love takes many forms, and amongst these pages you will experience all the complexities of emotion as you discover the ties that bind a man to a woman.

Code # 8229 • Quality Paperback • $9.95

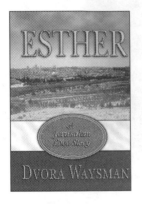

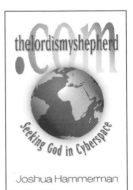

thelordismyshepherd.com
By Joshua Hammerman

thelordismyshepherd.com opens a new and necessary dialogue on the soul of cyberspace. It will change the way you think about your computer, about God, about the future and about the interconnected destiny of humanity in this ever-shrinking world.

Code #8210 • Quality Paperback • $10.95